DUCK DOGS

DUCK DOGS

All About the Retrievers

Richard A. Wolters

Foreword by Gene Hill

DUTTON  NEW YORK

DUTTON

Published by the Penguin Group
Penguin Books USA Inc.,
375 Hudson Street, New York, New York, U.S.A. 10014
Penguin Books Ltd,
27 Wrights Lane, London W8 5TZ, England
Penguin Books Australia Ltd,
Ringwood, Victoria, Australia
Penguin Books Canada,
2801 John Street, Markham, Ontario, Canada L3R 1B4
Penguin Books (N.Z.) Ltd.,
182–190 Wairau Road, Auckland 10, New Zealand

Penguin Books Ltd, Registered Offices:
Harmondsworth, Middlesex, England

First published by Dutton,
an imprint of Penguin Books USA Inc.
Published simultaneously in Canada
by Fitzhenry & Whiteside Limited.

First printing, April 1990

1 3 5 7 9 10 8 6 4 2

Library of Congress Cataloging-in-Publication Data

Wolters, Richard A.
Duck dogs: all about the retrievers/Richard A. Wolters. — 1st
ed.
p. cm.
Includes index.
ISBN 0-525-24477-8
1. Retrievers. 2. Duck shooting. I. Title.
SF429.R4W596   1990
636.7'52—dc20   89-16823
*   CIP*

Printed in the United States of America

Designed by REM Studio

Diagrams by Kirk Burns unless otherwise indicated

To my hunting buddy,
TAR

Contents

Foreword

Remember the Saturday afternoon serials in the movies and how when something bad was about to happen to the hero some kid (often my little brother) would shout, "Look out behind you!"

Any of us who know and respect Richard Wolters have to applaud the fact that here is a man who has had the courage and insight to stop us every so often to shout, "Look out behind you!" Richard has devoted much of his career to gun dogs, retrievers in the main—and more than a lot of this work has been done in an effort not only to improve the breeds and standards, but also, oddly enough, to keep well-meaning folks from ruining them.

Wolters is the ultimate iconoclast. He doesn't necessarily believe *anything* until he is satisfied, through his own research, that it is so. When, many years ago, Richard and I were trialing our first Labradors, he was dissatisfied with the training books. The old guard dismissed him as just another newcomer. Wrong! His book *Water Dog*—a revolutionary rapid training method—has become a bible—with incredible sales to back it up. Everyone said it was already known where the original retrievers got started—wrong again! Wolters found differently and wrote about it with charm and humor. And, when Richard and a few others rightly became disenchanted with the field-trial procedures, guess what happened? Right—they came up with an entirely new set of standards and rules and created the North American Hunting Retriever Association. And the average retriever owner has come to love it; it has been good for him and great for his gun dog.

The point of this reprise is to remind you that Wolters has been the best friend our retrievers have had in a long time—maybe ever. And this book is the one that puts the best of all these projects under one cover. I have to call it his *magnum opus*. Here we dispel the myths of breed histories, training methods, and the future of our retrievers. But Richard doesn't stop there. He isn't satisfied to say that this or that is wrong; he goes on to tell you what's right—and *how* you can do it and *why* you should do it.

To paraphrase a fairly recent title, this book tells you everything you wanted to know about your retriever but didn't know whom to ask.

You'll no doubt find things here that you disagree with—but that's Wolters's way as well. He wants you to learn to challenge the ordinary. I disagree with some of the things Richard says too—but his point is to make us think, for the good of the sport. (For the good of this sport I wish he'd buy a better grade of Scotch whisky—and I haven't won that argument either. . . .)

I know there will be other books on retrievers and their goals and their training, as there should be. But I strongly doubt that any of them will really add much to what you have right here. There's a small inscription on one of the gates at Harvard College: "Enter here to grow in wisdom." This timeless hope would make a marvelous subtitle for this book.

GENE HILL

Why This Book?

If this were a mystery novel, with the setting in a duck marsh, I wouldn't dare start the preface and tell you who done it or how the book ends.

But this book is not fiction. It's very factual and will even contain history. I will also make some predictions. In fact, I will make one right now. Our retrievers, especially the Labradors, are safe from the raids made upon these breeds by the show people and breeders for those big pet-market bucks. It was getting mighty close—almost touch and go. This story could have turned out entirely differently. When you get to the end of the book, you too will feel comfortable that we stopped the who done it before our hero, the working retriever, was killed off.

We know who tried to kill Cock Robin! Simple, my dear Watson. It was all solved with a little logic and clairvoyance. We closely examined the handwriting on the wall, and the evidence appeared clear. Simple deduction from the victim's statistics explained the crime in progress, and the culprits were identified. Timing was a prime factor. Scotland Yard was not called in because action by the vigilantes stopped the rascals in their tracks.

Now, if you understand all that, know the facts and history behind all this, you won't have to go on and read to solve this mystery. Otherwise, read on, and the story will be unfolded for you.

Still, we must keep alert to be sure the future progeny of our hunting retrievers is safe, which is something the hunter can't claim for many breeds, such as the Cocker Spaniel or the Irish Setter.

This book will show you, once you understand the problem, how you can become a part of this anticrime program and have a lot of fun, and your dog is going to love it. It could even be a thriller. History will show you that this is the first time a hunting dog that became popular in the general dog market has survived the embarrassment of quickly becoming a non-hunter—a dud.

If you're a hunter, you have the noble responsibility, once you examine the facts contained here, of becoming the protector of your dog's progeny. Just having a puppy registered with a dog registry, AKC or UKC, or Scotland Yard itself, is only a stab at guaranteeing that it is purely bred of hunting stock. Today, such certificates mean almost nothing about a young puppy's hunting ability.

Progeny from proven working stock solves the case. With a good working retriever, it is not going to take a Sherlock Holmes to deduce how to increase your game bag. You will have a dog that can do it all itself.

It has been brought to the hunting public's attention that their retrieving dogs were headed for serious problems. Historically, we have seen that hunting dogs popular with the general public lose their hunting ability. In recent times, the retriever's popularity with nonhunters has exploded both here and in Britain. Labs and Goldens in particular were in jeopardy. This brought about a resurgence of interest in our working retrievers.

The response to the call to save our hunting retrievers has been overwhelming.

Now, with all this newfound interest in our hunting retrievers, it's the purpose of this book to tell their story, from beginning to end. It's a fascinating story that takes us back many centuries. Piece by piece, we will weave it all together.

History, however, is not the whole story here. It's just the vehicle we will use so the hunter will understand his place in time in keeping our retrievers out of trouble. My second purpose is to show you how to get your retriever into the mainstream of the new action. This is not a basic training book, but Chapter 7 is a "how to" for retriever field *tests*.

The organization that ramrodded the whole new movement in this country is the North American Hunting Retriever Association. Once you understand its purpose, and the purpose of other organizations that have followed the NAHRA lead, you will see how they have worked to ensure our retrievers' future. We're hoping you and your dog will want to "get into the act."

The work of NAHRA should in no way be confused with the American Kennel Club's licensed field trials. Instead, NAHRA's field tests are used to assess the dogs against written hunting standards, and dogs are judged in field situations that follow those standards. These field tests are not a competition between dogs; their purpose is to find the dogs that can do the work the hunter requires, no matter where he lives. The standards are truly national. The dog is required to show in the field tests that it could work on any or all of our North American game birds. The field tests simulate conditions and settings as closely to real hunting situations as possible.

The history of our retrievers, besides being informative and often fascinating, will demonstrate how important this new movement is for our dogs. Then we will show you how you and your dog can join the movement. We'll show you what will be required of your dog and how to set up tests to teach it what it must know to become a working, hunting retriever. The field tests are divided into three categories: Started, Intermediate, and Senior. We will take you up the rungs of the ladder.

RICHARD A. WOLTERS
Hanover, Virginia

1

Some
Background

The starting assumption of this book is that our most popular hunting retrievers, the Labrador and the Golden, until recently were very close to being on the endangered species list. Our story will show how they are in the process of being saved. It is practically an accomplished fact now, but if I allow you to believe this is so, you might not think it important to read on and understand just what has happened to your dog. Knowing the facts is not only interesting but will enable you, the hunter, to make decisions to prevent this situation from ever arising again.

Most animals get on the endangered species list because for one reason or another their population has decreased. Then we sign petitions to save the whale, and the whooping crane, and go to Ducks Unlimited dinners to save our waterfowl. But the white-tail deer, in certain areas, is in just as much trouble, and *its* problem is overpopulation. This is similar in part to the story of the Lab and Golden, but this is not so for the other major hunting retriever in the United States, the Chesapeake Bay Retriever.

The Chessie and Lab—
Something in Common

Let's take a look first at the Chessie, for I believe it will shed some light on the problem. The Chesapeake Bay Retriever, much like the Labrador Retriever, is a dog that was developed out of necessity for specific work. The Lab was developed in Newfoundland and the Chessie on our own Eastern Shore. This all happened before the day of national kennel clubs and dog registries. Like most of our hunting breeds, the dogs were "put together" before the day of standards by men who either understood breeding or by hit and miss stumbled onto the right mix. You will see that the Golden is a perfect example of this process. The English for centuries were masters at breeding animals for a specific purpose, be it horses, cattle, or dogs. The science of genetics wasn't even heard of, but generations of experience—a dash of this and a spot of that—produced, they hoped. We, of course, will never know about the cases where this "science" of hit-and-miss breeding messed up, but if it did, the mix was changed until it *did* work.

Neither the Chessie nor the Lab was developed genetically by that kind of British know-how. In the case of the Labrador, the second time it entered England, in the early 1800s, it arrived with its abilities and temperament already set. The dog that came down to us as the Labrador was owned by the landed gentry and lived in large kennels, so the breed was kept pure. The dog had to be well mannered and easily controlled. It was a social animal and hunted under man's direction. For these qualities and because of its outstanding new work in Britain as a hunter, the dog was prized throughout the whole of the nineteenth century by its great benefactors, the earls of Malmesbury and the dukes of Buccleuch. These men were responsible for bringing the Labrador into the twentieth century. Interestingly, their appreciation was silent and did not reach the public ear until the end of the nineteenth century.

The starting point for the Chessie is the same as for today's Labrador. Two Newfoundland water dogs (one of the names the Labrador was known by at the beginning of the nineteenth century) were rescued in the Chesa-

A drawing of the Chesapeake from the last century

peake Bay along with the crew of a sinking English brig. The vessel, bound from Newfoundland for Poole Harbor, England, carried codfish and was to take on a partial load of lumber in the Chesapeake Bay area. The two pups aboard, Sailor, the male, and the female Canton, named for the ship that saved crew and dogs, became the foundation of the Chesapeake Bay Retriever breed. The year was 1807. Cod-fishing vessels returning from Newfoundland were the means by which the Labrador entered England from Newfoundland. These two pups were sidetracked. Interestingly, 1807 is just two years before the first record in England of the Labrador's hunting skills was written down. So, both breeds were developed for hunting at the same time.

The Chessie was developed first by a handful of sportsmen, farmers on both the eastern and the western shores of the Chesapeake. Writers on the

Chessie all make educated guesses at what dogs were bred to Sailor and Canton to make today's dog. It wasn't just luck that the Newfoundland water dog working instincts remained so dominant throughout the Chessie's development. It was Charles Darwin who commented, while doing a study on the big Newfoundland dog, on the dominant genes that would result when breeding took place on an isolated island. Indeed Newfoundland was isolated. There was no dog on the island until the British started fishing there in the late fifteenth century. The Lab has very dominant genes.

A Breed and Personality Are Developed

The credit for the development of the Chessie in the early nineteenth century goes to the Eastern Shore farmers, but almost immediately the breed was taken over by the Chesapeake watermen—the market hunters and oystermen. Their needs were different from those of the prosperous farmers. It is doubtful that the watermen of the Eastern Shore knew any of the fine points of breeding. They needed the workaholic ability of this new dog, but they had to add the protective instinct, as we will see later. The Chessie fitted the bill. The watermen most likely developed the dog the same way the sheepherders of Scotland produced the great working Border Collie. They knew the best dogs in their vicinity, and when the time came they bred the best and skipped over the others. Indications are that the watermen stumbled into their success the same way. They were not breeders of other animals. They were not well educated and didn't have any sources of outside help. It is important to our story that both dogs, the Lab and the Chessie, were developed and used extensively by extremely poor, uneducated fishermen.

Both the watermen of the Eastern Shore and the fishermen of Newfoundland were outcasts from the mainstream of society. Both groups were hardy, tough men.

There was one major difference between them, and that difference is reflected in their dogs. The Newfoundland fishermen sailed out of Poole, England, and worked for large trading companies. They were not allowed

The Chessie is a powerful dog. *(A. H. Rowan, Jr., Photo)*

to live in Newfoundland, only to work there during the fishing season. They were little more than indentured servants. They were illiterate and owned nothing except the clothes on their back and the few possessions they carried with them. They lived in miserable conditions with their shipmates and worked in teams of four with a dog. It was a dreary life, but there was little danger of their losing their possessions, a matter of constant concern for the watermen. The fisherman worked long hours and in return received little more than a subsistence living. His reward was a small lump sum when he returned to England each autumn. As for his dog, he used it but didn't own it. The dog was left behind each autumn, at the end of the fishing season, for the winter work crews to use for their survival hunting. By sheer breeding luck, the Lab's working instincts have been unparalleled, but there was no need to develop a protective instinct in the dog, because he worked for many masters and none of them had anything to protect.

It All Started in England

The original dog that ended up as the Labrador was taken from England to Newfoundland in the sixteenth century by the men of Devon, poor woods-men who eked out a living in the forests and were recruited by the fishing industry for their woodsmanship and survival skills to be the repair men for the cod-fishing fleet after the fishermen left in the autumn. They were a small group of men known as the "winter work crews." Originally, they took their hunting dog from home because they had to sustain themselves by hunting through the bitter winter while repairing the equipment. In the spring they went back to England, and "their" hunting dogs stayed and were then used by the fishermen. Contrary to the popular story, the dogs did not swim the net lines, as the early historians suggested, because you do not catch cod on the surface with nets. The fish were taken by bottom fishing using long lines festooned with hundreds of hooks. The dog's job, spring, summer, and autumn, was working the fishing dories. The cod or halibut were brought to the surface from the depths, became disoriented, and often thrashed off the hooks. The dogs went overboard and retrieved those fish. Over a period of almost three hundred years, the dogs worked for men who were poor and illiterate. They owned nothing—not even the dogs.

The Eastern Shore's Watermen

The waterman of the Eastern Shore was a different sort of social outcast. He was a loner, and his dog was a loner with him. His dog came from the same stock the Newfoundland fisherman had developed from the hunting dog brought across the Atlantic by the woodsmen from Devonshire. The waterman lived in a shack on one of the bays or marshes, and his dog slept outside on a pile of rags. The waterman's worldly possessions were his boat, fishing gear, guns, and the dog that guarded him and his scanty belongings. His oyster beds he protected to the point of war; if need be both man and dog fought side by side. The loner's dog did not get to associate with other dogs or other people. The shack had to be guarded against those who might steal the gear while the waterman was off delivering his oysters or ducks to the market. The dog was his sheriff. For over a hundred years, the Chessie was

Teddy Roosevelt and cronies become part of the growing sport of waterfowl hunting. Photographed in the early 1900s at Marling Farms Gunning Club on Kent Island, Maryland. *(Photo from* Waterfowler's World, *October–November 1986)*

bred for this work. He became the toughest retrieving dog ever. His daily job made the work of the sportsman's dog look like child's play.

In the late nineteenth and early twentieth centuries, outdoor sports became a favorite pastime for many Americans, especially the more affluent. The Chessie was taken into the waterfowler's blind, not only on the Eastern Shore of the Chesapeake but from coast to coast; it was one of the few sporting dogs to be developed in America. There was one drawback to the dog. Although its work was spectacular, because of its breeding for the waterman's protective needs, it was a one-man dog, hardheaded and therefore hard to train and handle. In social situations, it was somewhat unreliable.

A New Dog Shows Up in America

During the early part of this century, the American waterfowler's favorite dog was without any doubt the Chesapeake Bay Retriever. In the early 1920s, however, another dog began trickling into the United States, from England, the Labrador. In England the Lab had the aristocracy as its benefactors; in America it was the wealthy. The dog's easy temperament and outstanding hunting abilities made it a favorite with the upper classes, but its numbers remained relatively small.

As we shall see later, a fluke not only saved the Labrador from an early demise in the United States but catapulted the dog into such popularity that today it is the number-one hunting dog in the country and number two in all breed popularity . . . but this is not a happy situation.

The reasons the Lab became so popular are obvious. The American sportsman, like the waterman, needed a strong retriever, but he didn't need such a hardheaded, overprotective dog as the Chessie in his family. The honest and hardworking Lab, with the baby-sitter personality, became king for both the waterfowler and the upland hunter. From there the Lab became a "station wagon" dog. As Americans moved to the suburbs, they took a Labrador with them because of his easy manner.

Popularity Has Its Effect

All of this caused serious problems for both retriever breeds, and both have suffered, but for opposite reasons. The Chesapeake's popularity faded considerably. Actually, that should be stated another way. In the late 1930s, America started to become very pet conscious, and there developed a breeding business to supply the growing pet market. The Chessie didn't become one of the fashionable dogs, in spite of the fact that it is one of the few native American breeds. It also lost out seriously in the duck marsh, where more and more hunters took on the "new fellow on the block," the Labrador. Some Chessie breeders seem to have developed a chip on their shoulder about the place their dog was relegated to in the canine world. Actually they should be pleased.

Fads Take Their Toll

The public develops fads in dogs, and this has been very true with the Labrador. In this country in the 1950s, the yellow Labrador started to become popular in the pet market. It took ten or more years for this really to take its toll. Breeders started breeding for color because the yellow dog brought a higher price. Breeding for color alone and ignoring the work aspect of the dogs soon produced a line of dogs that looked good in the show ring and couldn't do a thing in the field. In the 1970s, the chocolate Lab was the next fad, and the prices were even higher. This color was just a narrower slice of the recessive yellow gene. To get these dogs, breeders went farther and farther from the work side of the Lab and produced a dog that in most cases is useless in the field.

Today, for the hunter to get a yellow or chocolate Lab that can hunt, he must naturally get it from working stock. Until recently, finding working stock was quite a problem for the hunter. The pet and show markets had become so big that the hunter had no real way of knowing what he was buying. Sticking to the black Labs seemed to help to some degree, but soon even that variety was dominated by the show dog. Breeding for a show standard, with no real consideration for the dog's work, will only lead to trouble. Show breeders gave lip service to their desire to keep the "work" in the breed, but had no real idea how to do it.

The Lab and Chessie Have Opposite Problems

We will develop the whole story as we progress, but at this juncture in the story, at the beginning of the 1980s, we found our hunting retrievers in a serious situation. The Chessie's numbers and popularity had faded because of its hardheadedness and overprotective personality. The Labrador was overpopular because of its baby-sitter personality and biddability in training.

The Chessie, because of its reduced numbers, never got into the trouble the Lab was facing. It never became a target for the pet market. Although there were some breeders who were trying to "improve" its personality, it was at the cost of sacrificing the dog's work. That's the sort of thing show breeders don't seem to understand.

The Hunter's Dilemma

But the Labrador, now the second most popular dog in the country, was being swallowed up by the show and pet markets. For the average hunter to try to find good working stock was like playing Russian roulette. The

Through breeding and improved training methods, gigantic strides in performance have been made. August Belmont's dog Super Chief did more for the Labradors than any other dog. *(Courtesy of August Belmont, Jr.)*

dilemma for the hunter was brought on forty years ago when the AKC left the hunter sitting way out in left field with no place in their operation. By the early 1980s, he had just about lost control over his dog.

A Great Worker, but
Too Few Dogs for the Hunter

In spite of this great surge in popularity, the United States still has the best working retrievers in the world, thanks to a few very select trainers in this country. There is no question in my mind that if there were a World Series of retrievers, our second team would cream the opposition no matter where it came from—England, the Continent, South Africa, Canada, or Australia. In very short order, through breeding and improved training methods practiced by a very select few licensed field trialers, their dogs have made gigantic strides in performance. The work that would have earned a dog the title of National Champion in this country a decade earlier wouldn't get that dog into the running today. The work the outstanding dog, Shed of Arden, did fifty years ago would be child's play for today's good young dog.

The highly competitive game of field trials was for the rich man, and that cut out most of the hunters. The problem was that with only two thousand field trialers in the country, they couldn't supply the puppy needs each year for the millions of hunters.

The Dilemma?

While giant strides were being made by the field-trial people in the development of the hunting work of our retrievers, an even larger segment of the retriever-owning public, the show people and breeders, were undoing by default all that the field trialer was accomplishing. The breeder and show community hustled to meet the exploding demands of the pet market. Priorities seemed to get mixed up, or the buck got in the way. But the real culprit was the American Kennel Club—it did not police what was happening and almost allowed a breed to go down the drain in the name of dog fancy.

Our retrievers are not unique in that regard: the history of every hunting dog that has become popular through the AKC show ring is the same— the dog has lost its working ability. The key to the problem is popularity. For example, the most popular dog in the country is the Cocker Spaniel. Once a great hunting dog, today the Cocker is useless in the field. It can't hunt its way to the meat counter in a supermarket. The Poodle was number two. It has been taken out of the duck marsh and made into a sissy. Its topknot is dressed in ribbons. The AKC English Setter's silky coat, down to its knees, would be ruined in a brier patch, and it has lost its nose. The Irish Setter has been made into a highstrung, blooming idiot. The list goes on. If the men who started the AKC one hundred years ago could see what their organization has done to our hunting and also to our working dogs, they would turn over in their graves.

The retriever story is not just two-sided (field trials and dog shows)—it has three parts. The original guy in the picture in the first place was the hunter, a fact the AKC forgot about. Sixty years after the Labrador was introduced into this country, he found himself sitting on the sidelines. The show people and the field-trial people took control of the dog under the banner of the AKC. The hunter was left without even knowing where to get a pup from good hunting stock that he could depend on.

Simply speaking, by 1980, the AKC, which controlled the dog game in this country, divided the activity into two categories, the show ring and field trials, and there was no place for the hunter and his dog. The hunter was not interested in the show ring and couldn't afford the field-trial game. Without an organization, the hunters lost control of their dog. They had no way of knowing who hunted in the next county, let alone what dogs they had.

Where was the Chessie during all this? Because of the dog's "unpopularity," which is its good luck, this problem is not going to rear its ugly head with the Chessie. There is not enough money in the Chessie market for the show ring to ruin that dog. Yet even so, some of the show people are trying. In order to breed a better temperament into the Chessie for the pet-market dollar, breeders will have to sacrifice the dog's workability, and that isn't going to help the dog, especially for the reader of this book who wants a hunting retriever. The Chessie people should let well enough alone.

NAHRA Brings the Hunter Back Where He Belongs

In the early 1980s, the hunters became fed up with this situation and bucked the system. They started their own organization, the North American Hunting Retriever Association (NAHRA), to gain back the control they had lost. NAHRA has been very successful. Its work has now become a coast-to-coast operation. Already it has accomplished its main mission. The Labrador is no longer on the endangered species list. The hunter's dog is safe. And there is no longer a concern about what the show people do that can harm our retrievers. Now the attitude among hunters is "Let them do what they want." There is a working breeding program in operation for the hunters' dogs, and now the hunter can know exactly where to turn to get his puppy stock.

2

A Touch of the Queen

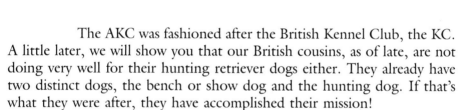

The AKC was fashioned after the British Kennel Club, the KC. A little later, we will show you that our British cousins, as of late, are not doing very well for their hunting retriever dogs either. They already have two distinct dogs, the bench or show dog and the hunting dog. If that's what they were after, they have accomplished their mission!

The English shooting literature is rich, but the only way really to understand the hunting retriever in England is to go over there and observe the good fellow in action. Pheasant shooting in England and Scotland is something we Americans read and dream about but few get the opportunity to experience. So the trip I made recently had a twofold purpose: to shoot the esteemed British pheasant and to witness the National Championship of the International Gun Dog League.

First the Championship

In early December each year the British hold their equivalent of our National Retriever Championship. It's run by the British International Gun Dog League.

I have attended a number of English trials and have seen this Championship twice. The first time I saw their National, eight years ago, I was not impressed with their dogs. I had little to say back then about the dog work because I was a guest. But I thought the judging was terrible and the dogs that won placements in the event were worse than terrible. This time I was over there on my own, and the purpose was to observe more closely and give the British dog a second chance. Was that first National I had seen just a bad show or were the British in general not performing up to their ability?

I've concluded that the work the British dogs do might be okay for the English, Irish, Welsh, and Scots, but that their dogs would be useless in our country.

First, you must understand that the British are great sportsmen who definitely enjoy their dogs and the work the dogs do for them in the field. But their own traditionalism gets in the way of the development of their retrievers. We ask more of a year-old pup than they do of their National Champion. Field trials for retrievers started in England in 1902, and in this year's National they were doing exactly the same thing in the same way as their grandfathers had done it.

My major complaint is first, they only scratch the surface of the real potential of the retrievers. Some might argue that we have taken our dogs, in only fifty-five years, too far in our AKC Licensed Field Trials, but that is why we have the North American Hunting Retriever Association (NAHRA) in this country. We are testing our dogs against a working, hunting standard. Believe me, there was not one dog in the British national event that could pass the NAHRA Senior standard—not one!

They Do
and They Don't

It is not as if the dogs are not fine animals, but the British don't give their dogs a chance. They don't ask their dogs in their championship to do even a double retrieve and a triple would be unheard of! They never ask the dogs to do a blind retrieve or even take a line, and require hardly any water work. They don't ask the dogs to quarter the field or to find and flush the game. With all those don'ts, what do their dogs do?

The dogs walk at heel, and a line of hunters and beaters flush the game. Many birds that sit tight are missed, walked over by those in the hunting line. Those birds flush behind the line of hunters. In my eye, this is dangerous hunting. As the line moves forward, the guns must swing through 180 degrees to shoot, not a comfortable feeling for others in the line.

Here is what makes up their National. It's in two parts. In the first part, called the walk-up, as many as forty people form a line across a beet field. It consists of four dog handlers, each with a dog, four judges, eight guns, a gamekeeper, a few photographers and writers, and about twenty beaters. The beaters carry sticks and beat the cover in front of them as the line moves forward. When a bird is flushed, the line stops. If the bird is down, the judge decides which dog shall run. This is a single retrieve, usually at about thirty to sixty yards. Each dog gets two chances, and then that dog is retired and another comes into the line. The important part of this British game is that if a dog cannot find the bird in a reasonable period of time, another dog is given a chance. If the second dog gets the bird, the first one is said to have had its eye wiped and is out of the running. They do this for a day and a half, moving from field to field. That is 90 percent of the trial. The whole business revolves around short single retrieves. A big part is played in this game by the "runner," or wounded bird. The dog must track and trail such a bird. The British make a big thing of this, something our hunting dogs do because it comes built in. Their mommies and daddies gave them that ability. It's not something you can put into a dog by training.

(ABOVE) There are two parts to a British trial. The walking line flushes the game. The game is shot, and the judges ask one dog at a time to retrieve . . .
(BELOW) . . . The dogs are lined up. Birds are driven over the dogs and shot. After all the gunning action is over, the dogs, one at a time, make the retrieve. (*Author Photos*)

The Gallery Loved It

Let me set up a situation I saw. The gallery walks behind a flag bearer on the side of the field. They move along with the line. I spent part of the time in the line and part in the gallery. In this particular walk-up situation, the gallery had a better view of the action than the guns, the handlers, or the judges. A bird was flushed and shot. It landed in a dip and was only stunned. The bird got up and ran to the wall in front of the gallery and up over a knoll, where it took refuge in a bush. The first dog missed the trail, and that was the end of it. The second dog was handled to the spot where the bird had fallen. It picked up the scent and followed the trail to the wall, then up over the knoll to the bird. When it returned, the gallery applauded.

Of course it was a nice piece of trailing, but if I were the judge I would have dropped the dog and put it out of the competition. To get to the area of the fall from the handler's side, some forty yards, the dog had ten whistle refusals. The dog paid no heed to the whistle and literally stumbled into the area of the fall after about eight to ten minutes of hacking by the handler with no response from the dog. Any good retriever should, quickly and with dispatch, be able to follow the handler's hand directions to the fall and track the scent from there.

The British do not teach a dog to take a line, which would have worked well in the above situation. Show one of our good dogs the direction you want it to go in, and it will run "to Philadelphia" as straight as an arrow and won't stop until it has found scent or hears the handler's whistle. The British do not know how to train a dog to take casts . . . either back or to the side. When I've asked their best trainers why they don't use some of the systems set down in the literature by many Americans, the answer is "We don't do it that way. It's not our tradition."

My second complaint is that the British have their priorities mixed up. The most important thing to them is that the dog must walk at heel without being spoken to and without making a sound. This is truly a display of fantastic manners. Manners is really their whole game. And it has been explained to me over and over that the dog should not interfere in any way with the shooter. A whine or a break would be disaster. Their dogs sit at a drive with birds falling all around, and they look as if they couldn't care less . . . as if they are in a different world.

Their priorities are mixed up. We have found in our country that the retrievers are the best of all the flushing dogs. It just makes sense to me to have the birds found and flushed in front of the walking guns—not behind. And besides, dogs do a better job of rooting out birds than man can do! Use them that way and you'll flush more birds, which is really what hunting is all about. If I had my druthers, I'd have a dog that showed interest, and a whine or so would not bother me if I had a good trade-off. If that dog went out with dispatch and made the retrieve so I could get on with the shooting, I'd be very happy. The cost of shooting pheasant in England or Scotland for a week is the price of a new car. I would be more aggravated giving up shooting time as the line comes to a halt until the bird is retrieved and having to wait there because of the ineffectual handling and response of the dog. It would be more important to me to have fast, crisp retrieves than to worry if the dog whined out of excitement.

Because of tradition, they won't teach their dogs to handle crisply, so they have produced a well-mannered, silent dog, who, when it comes to handling, wastes the gunners' time and that means money and birds. This is the upland hunter's equivalent of the sport of waterfowl hunter, who also wants the birds picked up with dispatch and dog back in the blind so they can get on with the hunting. It was Lee Wulff, America's outstanding fly fisherman and teacher, who said, "You never catch trout while you are false casting."

The British do a second kind of test in their trials—*pass shooting*. They have birds driven by beaters over guns who stand at a butt and shoot the birds as they fly overhead. The dogs sit by their handlers until all the birds are shot. When I asked the British hunters why they waited, in these driven shoots, until the drive was over before the dogs were sent to make the retrieves, their answers were based on tradition. This was the way they had always done it. No dog is going to remember where fifty birds had fallen. Why not allow the dogs to retrieve as the birds fall? Why give a crippled bird a half hour's head start before the dog is sent?

In this country, at many of our better shooting clubs, we have a game similar to the British driven shoot. We call it *tower shoot*. The guns, about a dozen or more, stand at positions in a large circle around a "tower." The tower, some eighty feet high, is where five hundred or one thousand birds are released, one or two at a time. The tower gives a bird a fast start, and the guns, at a good distance, shoot the fast-flying birds as they pass overhead. Retrievers and their handlers stand behind the perimeter and retrieve the birds as they fall in their segment. In no way does it bother the guns, who are shooting high shots, nor does it put the dog in jeopardy as in the case of flushed birds.

Yes, the British priorities are mixed up: they put more emphasis on manners for the "comfort" of the hunter than on the work of the hunt.

What's Behind
the "Tradition"

I believe I finally have come to understand where the British ideas for their hunting retrievers came from and where they went wrong. It all started back in the Victorian era when the sport of shooting driven birds began. I will delve into this in detail shortly, but for the moment let me just say that one thing becomes clear from the early writings. The sport of pass shooting driven birds took tremendous concentration. It was documented that Lord Ripon once had seven dead birds in the air at one time! The record was well over a thousand birds a day. That takes concentration. A dog who made as much as a noise or a break would be guilty of an unforgivable sin. I got the distinct feeling from the literature that these men cared about one thing, and one thing only—shooting and killing in high numbers. That was the game of the day. The best books I have found on the history of the sport of driven birds never even mention the dogs or their work.

The dog was just one part of the "show," along with literally an army of beaters. The gamekeeper was the general. The gamekeeper's gillies handled the dogs. Dogs and workers alike were kept in their place. Although that era is now over and past, through tradition, the old attitude toward the work of the dog has never changed. The dog had to keep its place. This meant absolute silence, and it never moved or made a retrieve until the drive was over, a rather stupid requirement if retrieving the birds was an important part of the game. As a result of all this, the British to this day just never have asked much of their dogs, except fantastic manners. As if the Marquis of Ripon were still at the butt.

As I watched the walk-up in the beat field, where one dog worked at a time retrieving single falls for the gun, it was hard for me to realize this was their National Championship; these were the top thirty-two dogs in Great Britain. The first day seventeen of them could not find a bird flushed and down thirty to sixty yards in front of the line, a simple single retrieve. We'd send dogs like that to the show ring.

Walking the beat fields and watching a day and a half's worth of single retrieves gets to be slow going. But I was assured that the last event, a driven shoot over water, would be spectacular. There were only seven dogs left for this event. It took place on the bank of a lake where the woods came down to within thirty yards of the water. The seven dogs sat in line about five feet from the edge of the lake, facing the woods. Three guns stood with the dogs and handlers. The birds were driven out of the woods and flown over the dogs. About a dozen birds were dropped. I was shocked to see that if a bird was hit and sailed onto the far side of the water, only sixty to eighty yards away, a pickup dog was stationed there to get those birds. I asked the reporter for the *Shooting Times* why they were doing the pickup, and he suggested that the judges thought it too far—too much of a swim!

When the judges had seven birds in the water about ten to thirty yards offshore, the guns stopped shooting. One at a time the dogs were sent. One dog swam its twenty yards puppy style. The dogs were given only one water retrieve. I felt at least two of the dogs would have refused a second entry because it was cold water. If the dead bird floated down the bank twenty or thirty yards on the wind, the handler was told to walk his dog down the shore until he was opposite the bird. Then the dog made a retrieve worthy of one of our five-month-old pups. But these were not puppies—these were the tested, best field dogs the British had.

Some time ago I was standing watching one of our NAHRA field tests, and a gentleman with a definite British accent was standing next to me. As a dog returned after a spectacular job, the man shook his head in amazement, half bit his lip, and turned to me and said, "You know, we English have introduced you colonists to all our sports, and then you turn around and show us how the game should be played." He thought for a moment and continued, "Another good example is that America's Cup. And now look at what *Stars and Stripes* did to one of our British cousins! You brought the cup home!"

We have a group of retriever people in this country who are enamored of the British dog. I saw some of these AKCers in action on this last trip. They feed the English a package of garbage about how cruel we are in our training. They think all Americans use electricity to "burn" their dogs or beer can openers on the dogs' ears to force-fetch. So the British have a terribly confused idea about what is really taking place on the retriever scene in America.

British Judges in America

Another thing that bothers me is that AKC show people are always importing English judges who know nothing about our needs in a retriever to judge our dogs. I think our people feel that the imported judges with their charming English accents bring with them a small piece of the Queen. Then the same judges sell their dogs here, "to give us better breeding stock." Seventeen of their top thirty-two dogs can't do a simple single retrieve???

My conclusion after seeing this National event and talking to a lot of people in Scotland, where the event was held, is that we all could benefit from a dialogue between the two countries. We could learn much about training for the manners their dogs possess, and they have much to learn about training for the actual field work. My honest feeling is that if they could forget their "traditions" and be objective about their dogs' work, they would have the most to gain from any such international discussions.

Importing retrievers into the United States is not new. Some thirty years ago a number of our top field-trial people imported finished field-trial champions from England. Not one of those dogs ever made the grade here—not one! Go back through pedigrees and you will not find any direct British blood in our top lines since the 1950s.

Yet the AKC is bringing in British judges to judge their hunting tests. There is no need to comment on that. I'd only get nasty.

I think that Gene Hill, who does a lot of shooting every year in Great Britain, states it all best: "The place for a British Labrador in England is on the left-hand front seat of a Jaguar."

The British are not stupid people by any means. They are conservative and traditionalists. To understand why this has gotten in the way of advancement in the training of their dogs, you really have to experience British shooting and the ambience of their game. You have to delve into the history of shooting in Britain to really understand their dog. Today they still play their game as they did in the Victorian period, but that period is gone.

The Victorian Era Invents Driven Shoots

Eighty years ago King Edward VII and his nine guests shot 2,728 pheasants in one day on his estate at Sandringham. This was only an average day of pass shooting at driven birds, a sport that developed during the Victorian era, starting about 1860. Previously, the aristocratic gentlemen walked through the fields and woods and shot pheasants flying away as the dogs flushed them to wing, as we did on my recent trip until the Scottish weather put an end to it. Back then, birds downed, in braces of only dozens, in a walk-up (or rough-shooting as the British call it today) was considered a most successful day afield. But the new Victorian sport of pass shooting sounded like bedlam and was warfare. Small armies of estate workers covered thousands of acres under the command of the gamekeeper, whose battle plan was a series of precisely timed, flanking maneuvers to encase the quarry and drive them toward the "cannon." Marlborough himself couldn't have prepared better plans of engagement to prevent an enemy from springing out of the trap. The "army" did the work; gentlemen "generals" gave the coups de grace. Thousands of driven pheasants were pushed ahead, then flushed toward the gentlemen, who stood at their "pegs" shooting fast-flying, head-on shots. Each shooter used at least a pair of guns and at least one loader, and at times as many as three. There was no moral issue about all this killing because the birds were raised for the table, and this was the means of the harvest. The sport required concentration but little physical

America imported the sport of bird shooting from England well over two hundred years ago. From William Henry Scott, *British Field Sports,* 1832.

effort. It was a simple arrangement, but the principle of the driven birds and the social consequences had a far-reaching effect. From all this evolved a life-style for the chosen that has rarely been duplicated in history.

Rough shooting—the sport of flushing game with dogs with a scatter-gun firing small shot for birds—has been a classic sport in England for two hundred years. We in America imported the sport, including their dogs, back in Revolutionary days. Little has been written or said about rough shooting once driven shooting took hold. The driven shoot overshadowed the sport of rough shooting because it had a major impact on the social, political, and economic life-style of England.

The stage was set for the newfangled sport of shooting driven birds, with its resultant social change, when Queen Victoria bought the Balmoral estate and took Scotland as her second home in the 1840s. The Consort, Prince Albert, a voracious deer hunter, gave the sport of stalking the Scottish red stag a royal acceptance. Scotland became the playground for the aristocrat and the new wealthy industrialist. Trains opened up the north country and great deerstalking estates were amassed. With the influx of the new wealth the devastated economy of Scotland, as a result of the defeat of Bonnie Prince Charlie in 1746, was rebuilt.

Whereas the sport of deerstalking was only two on one—the hunter and his stalker against the stag—the sport of driven birds entailed many, many hundreds of people. Actually, only eight or ten guns took part, but an army of workers were needed. The events were made into festive social occasions for the entourage. Hundreds of affluent people as well as workers became involved. The gallery, when not too bored with the whole affair, was made up of some of the most beautiful ladies of England and gentlemen of political and social position. This called for overflowing country-style house parties that included, besides the shooting, a full week of social activities. It was *the way* for all of the great landlords of rank in England to entertain during the autumn months. There were elaborate luncheons on the lawn, sumptuous dinner parties, gala costume balls, and some of the worst ever amateur stage productions written and acted by the bored ladies. These house parties became an elegant and costly entertainment obligation, causing bankruptcies among princes and lords alike. As the Grand Duchess of Mecklenburg-Strelitz exclaimed when she was informed that the emperor of

Sporting gentlemen used nets to capture the pheasant and the partridge. From the book *Gentleman's Recreation,* 1686.

Austria had accepted the invitation to attend a shoot, "What are we to do? Our poor palace only has sixty-two bedrooms."

The Prince of Wales, later King Edward VII, affectionately called Tum Tum, had neither the shape nor the temperament for the hard work of walk-up hunting. Rough shooting is rough going. But the prince had a passion for this newly organized driven shoot. That gave the sport the royal blessing in the social, political, and economic game of follow the leader. The railroads provided elaborately outfitted palaces on wheels that carried the guests to the country estates. The Prince of Wales had a station at Wolverton built specifically to accommodate his guests bound for Sandringham. Meanwhile, the development of the sporting gun enabled a small number of guns to bring down large numbers of birds. The "smart" Edwardians measured the success of the day in numbers. In 1913 King George V was disturbed by the nearly four thousand pheasant shot in a day, expressing his concern by saying "Perhaps we overdid it today."

British Traditions
Go Back into Time

The English monk Roger Bacon invented gunpowder in the thirteenth century, but it was not put to sporting use for many more centuries. Sporting gentlemen hunted the pheasant and partridge by hawking. Gunpowder in some cases was used for shooting nets to capture the game. It was not until the end of the eighteenth century that the flintlock muzzle loader was perfected to the point that flying game could be downed. It was still a difficult piece to fire: the sportsman had to remove the powder from a flask, ram a thick wad down the barrel, measure the shot from a pouch, ram a thin wad on top of the concoction, and then set the cap—and rain could ruin the whole operation. The hunter never held his left hand too far down the barrel when shooting such a contraption, for the barrel was likely to burst. The "hang fire" of the flintlock caused slow ignition of the powder and meant that a bird could be hit only if it was flying directly away from the hunter. A crossing shot was almost impossible. The shooter not only had to figure in the speed of the bird and the angle of flight, but also had to guesstimate the time for powder ignition. Try to figure out that lead in a split second! The bird had a good flying chance. But if, with the luck of St. Hubert, the bird did go down, the shooter could not see his success through the cloud of black powder smoke that erupted from the gun muzzle.

The principle of the percussion cap, which changed all that, was known for a long time; in fact, it's mentioned in Pepys's diary. It was not developed for fast shooting until the breech-loaded gun was invented in the 1850s. British jokes even today make sport of the fact that the gun is broken in half for fast loading. "O' Lor!" says the farmer, "he's bin and broken 'is gun the very firs shot!"

The famous gun makers of England, Purdey, Churchill, and Holland and Holland, to mention a few, developed guns over the next twenty years that have never been improved on. The principle of the cartridge was known, and the invention of smokeless powder in the 1880s made the full onslaught on British bird life possible.

That Era of Victorian Excess Has Now Passed

World War II hastened the social and economic changes. There is a new "aristocrat," the businessman. He's continuing where the old aristocracy left off. But things do not change radically in Great Britain; they evolve from tradition and need. The walk-up, or the rough shoot, where gentlemen with dogs flush their own game, is now being revised, not in the new way that we do it in America, but in the customary, traditional manner of Great Britain, and it's rather elegant.

Even the First Best-Seller Was on Hunting

There has never been a land revolution in England. Tradition has prevented it. The British aristocracy centuries ago set the standard for conduct and procedures for British hunting on the land. Today the new aristocracy is following the old customs. No society could ever do it again in the grand manner of the Victorian era, but they still perform their sport in elegant style. The arts of hunting and fishing have been a major part of British culture and traditions from before the time that the English language was put into print. Unlike the other cultures of Europe, when the printing press reached England in 1476, the first best-seller in the English language was not a religious book but a "how to" book on hunting.

By 1486 the nameless schoolmaster of St. Albans Abbey, who managed the printing press, had published eight books in Latin. Most of them have long since been forgotten except by scholars. His second book in the English language hit the jackpot and has stayed in print for five hundred years. It was printed from an earlier manuscript preserved at St. Albans. As the work had no earlier title, it was and is simply known as *The Boke of St. Albans.* The manuscript, written about 1450, dealt with hunting, hawking, and heraldry. It gave sensible advice in everyday language. Its sidelights on etiquette and the correct use of technical terms proved to be of substantial value to wealthy merchants who about the time of its publication began to mingle with the aristocracy. Ten years later a second printing of the book was enlarged to

Lieutenant Colonel Peter Hawker, author of *Instructions to a Young Sportsman,* the first book to mention the Labrador. This portrait appeared in the second edition of the book, 1830.

include a missing manuscript called a *Treatyse of Fysshynge wyth an Angle* (a remarkable explanation and how-to on fly fishing for trout), written by Dame Juliana Berners, prioress of Sopewell, a small nunnery just outside St. Albans. Poor but of noble birth, she may have been reared in the royal household of King Henry IV, where she perhaps learned her outdoor skills from, to quote her, "the right noble and full worthy prince the Duke of York, late called the Master of the Game." Scholars now attribute the whole of *The Boke of St. Albans* to Dame Berners. In the first one hundred years, 1486 to 1586, fourteen separate printings of the book were made. By 1814 there were twenty-four printings.

The same year brought another best-seller to the sportsman. It's called *Instructions to a Young Sportsman* and was written by Lieutenant Colonel Peter Hawker. This large work covers every facet of the shooting sports and became the bible for instructions and information. It covers and explains so much in such an easy manner that it has never been out of print. By 1844 it had had nine editions, and in 1846 received its first American printing. Hawker's son published two more editions after his father's death in 1859. Another edition was printed in Philadelphia in 1921. The latest printing is dated 1986. This book is to shooting what Izaak Walton's *Compleat Angler* is to fishing, a classic.

If the literature of a nation tells about its culture, shooting has hit the mark in Britain. There has been an overabundance of shooting literature. Every family of any social standing had a game book where any and all, generation after generation, could write and put their shooting prowess on record. In the early nineteenth century, even before Queen Victoria's reign, shooting was a major part of the rural scene, and London alone already supported sixty gun makers.

To an American hunter going to Scotland to partake of their game of rough shooting or walk-up shooting, it was interesting to observe that this sport, which is so old in Britain, is being played in the traditional manner even by the new society. The old aristocracy can no longer afford to hunt in their traditional way, but the businessman who has taken their place is playing the old game in style.

We in America have designed some rather ingenious guns. They are single barrels and both pump and automatic. Those used in certain types of hunting can fire as many as five shots. But the British rejected these newfangled, unsporting ideas. They used their traditional side-by-side, double-barrel shotgun (two shots). And if they wanted to shoot fast, they had their matching pair of guns and a loader to take the empty gun and hand the shooter a loaded one. Five shots from one gun was considered unsporting, but the Marquis of Ripon, that legendary great, once killed twenty-eight driven pheasants in one minute, and we have already told you about the seven dead birds in the air at once.

The other "big shot" was the sixth Lord Walsingham, who, in one day, August 30, 1888, bagged 1,075 grouse himself. The sport bankrupted him. Even today in British rough shooting the double-barreled is the only gun accepted, and by some, the later English invention of an over-and-under gun is frowned on. They won't even accept their own newfangled ideas.

Very few Americans had the opportunity to hunt in this Victorian game until the twentieth century. Money could not buy an invitation. It was an exclusive social activity that the British aristocracy kept for themselves. Many of the customs and traditions established well over one hundred years ago have persisted right up to today, in spite of the changes in the social structure.

The shooting costume became part of the tradition that has been passed down to today's shooter. The women, not that much a part of the actual hunting scene, wore no special outdoor clothes. As a houseguest for a week, it was considered bad form to wear the same gown more than once. Seven breakfast suits, usually of velvet or silk, were brought; then seven tweed outfits were needed for lunch with the guns and remaining afield afterward to observe the afternoon drives. That was followed by extravagant tea gowns and then seven formal satin or brocade evening dresses, plus a few costumes for the balls . . . along with seven everything elses. All this made a serious baggage problem, which the railroads solved by designing special baggage cars for these shooting house parties. Of course each family brought its valet and maids, who added to the housing problems. Taking one's wife on a shooting holiday could be rather expensive.

Early on the men wore tailcoats, waistcoats, and derbies in the field, but these were soon replaced by tweeds cut especially for the sport of shooting. The tailcoats were worn by the keepers until the practice developed of each estate using its own specially designed woolen plaid. Three-piece suits cut from the estate plaid, with vest, were part of the yearly pay of the keeper and key workers on the estate. This custom is still in effect. It's part of the tradition.

For the shooter, the Norfolk jacket became a very practical coat. Bi-

Women farmworkers, dressed in bloomers, making fun of the shooters dressed in knickers. A sketch from the Buccleuch family game book. (*Courtesy of the Duke of Buccleuch*)

swing cuts, box pockets, leather patches, and neck button adorned the sports jacket. Americans still giggle about the knickers, but they are the most practical form of leg covering if you have to negotiate briers. Going through even low underbrush or heather in long trousers is very inefficient and tiring. A humorous cartoon that was drawn in the duke of Buccleuch's family game book in the 1850s, shows women farmworkers coming upon shooters standing at their pegs. The women are making fun of the men dressed in "bloomers," and are showing off theirs.

The Scottish came up with the deerstalker hat; Sherlock Holmes wore one. It looks odd but it works: a peak in the front protects the eyes from the sun and the face from the rain; a peak in the rear keeps the water from running down one's neck; earflaps keep the ears warm; and a string keeps the whole contraption in place in a strong wind. It's not an inexpensive way to dress, necktie and all, but today British tradition still dictates that this is the costume! Meanwhile, the American cousin goes afield dressed like Paul Bunyan, looking a bit like a tramp. Banker or janitor, they dress alike.

Although the shooting sports in Britain appear as an in-place, ongoing affair, it is the gamekeeper who plays a most important role in keeping it all together. He has always been the unsung hero behind the scene. An act of Parliament in 1683 gave far-reaching powers to the gamekeeper, even to search and seize on suspicion to protect the land from poachers. By the late eighteenth century, Parliament had to intervene again because the landowners were using the statute to employ private armies under the guise of gamekeepers. Parliament then limited an estate to one gamekeeper, and a yearly fee for him and each dog was paid to the Crown.

After World War I wealthy Americans began receiving British invitations to join the game. Men like Jay Gould bought their own estates and also leased land in Britain. Gould turned the Farleyer House estate at Aberfeldy, Scotland, into a fine grouse-shooting moor. Others, Wall Streeters, enjoyed the British shooting so much that they imported the sport to America—the gamekeepers, the fine guns, the clothes, and even the dogs. It was a short-lived experiment. The Depression put a speedy end to it.

The day of the lavish shooting extravagances also came to an end in Britain. Most of the aristocracy and large landholders have come upon cash-flow difficulties. A well-run estate could manage about twelve driven shoots a year. The only way for the estates to continue the driven shoots was to lease most of the shooting days to the new aristocracy, the sporting businessmen. Possibly the landowner could afford to retain one or more days for his own use, but the day of two thousand brace of birds and the elegant house party was over.

Tradition Keeps the Sport as It Was in Victoria's Day

In other respects, tradition has not been abandoned. On driven bird shoots, although the number of birds has been greatly reduced, the procedures and ambience of the sporting part are much as they have always been. Also, the game is continued on a much-reduced scale by small landholders who put on an excellent day of sport for their friends and neighbors. Many syndicates have been formed to handle the high costs. The economic and social situation has brought a change that is very appealing to the American hunter. The walk-up, or rough shoot, is back in vogue on the big estates. Although some rough shooting has always been done by the small landowners, it was overshadowed by the driven shoot. Today the driven shoots have to be economically produced. As an important source of income, the rough shoot has come back into the game.

Here is the economic reason for the walk-up: a driven shoot scatters thousands of birds to the far corners of an estate. At fourteen pounds a head, it became the practice for the gamekeeper and a team of gillies to spend days after a shoot walking the estate, flushing the birds and flying all the stragglers back to the feeding pens. Now, because of the extra income it provides, rough shoots behind dogs are being sold to parties of guns. The estate workers no longer flush the game back to the feeding pens; the walk-up guns do it, paying for the privilege. They flush the game and move most of them back to the pens, shooting a very small percentage. Today, gamekeepers consider the original sport of rough shooting a very important part of game management.

Castle Living Is
Part of the Game

For one shoot I joined a group of English businessmen, who were kind enough to include me in their party. The plan was that we would meet at Borthwick Castle, eight or so miles south of Edinburgh and only a few miles from the Linwoods. The castle, built in 1430, has had its place in history. In 1567 Queen Mary of Scots sought sanctuary with her third husband, Lord Bothwell, in this impregnable fortress. They spent their last days of freedom here before being separated forever. Nearly a century later Oliver Cromwell besieged the castle, which led to the dethronement, trial, and beheading of the Stuart king, Charles I. The walls still bear the scars of the bombardment by Cromwell's cannon.

* * *

What an elegant beginning! Cocktails were served to our party of eight guns and their ladies before the twenty-foot open fireplace in what had to be the largest great hall in Scotland. Until modern times, this fireplace was the only source of heat in the whole of Borthwick Castle. You know how the mind can play games and do two things at once: in this case, I was holding my first conversations with the men I would be shooting with for the next few days, and at the same time I was being taken back to the day of Queen Mary. It was hard to believe that we were occupying the same space—and somehow I felt it was also the same time. Though I was answering the questions about the American woodcock and its miniature size in comparison to the British bird, my thoughts were racing. The long table in the great hall was set for our dinner. Plots for and against kings and queens had been hatched at this table. Major concerns and events of other days had been discussed here in the great hall, and now we were part of it, even if one does come to realize that being in the same "space" is possible, but being in the same "time" is impossible. Somehow this helps one understand the English sense of tradition a little better.

I had to laugh to myself because one of my new shooting companions had such a heavy cockney accent that I had difficulty understanding him at first. This, I thought to myself, is truly the new British "aristocracy," witty, well-read, elegantly dressed, obviously successful, and my new friend proved to be a hell of a fine shot. It was not so long ago that the cockney accent would never have been allowed on the trigger end of a shotgun. A gillie or possibly a beater? Yes! But not a gun.

I climbed, that first night, a circular stone staircase to my bedchamber high in the tower. The doorway was only four feet high. Whether it was still jet lag, or whatever, I lay awake in my stone room listening to the forty-mile-an-hour wind moaning against the window, which was only a slit cut into the twelve-foot-thick rock wall. I lay there wondering who before me had slept in this dungeonlike room. Who were they and what were their problems, their aspirations, their pleasures, or even their names?

The first morning at breakfast in the great hall, in Scotland, showed that tradition was still alive and well. Each man came to the table in his shooting tweeds and ate a hearty English breakfast.

The castle was a fun part of the ambience of the whole shooting experience. Each night there was a pleasant semiformal dinner, and on the last evening a banquet with pipers and all. Hearing the bagpipe wailing someplace deep in the walls of the castle was a moving experience.

A Memorable Experience

As I sat in the plane flying home to Virginia, I tried to put the Scottish experience into some sort of perspective. One major conclusion I came to as a Labrador Retriever buff was that the strong traditions of the British sportsmen had not helped in their retriever work. In fact they had hindered it. Labradors became part of this affair of driven shoots as pickup dogs, back in the last century. But in Britain the dogs were considered a very insignificant part of the sport. They were a necessity like the beaters and other workers.

The English did not start to test and field-trial their retrievers until 1902. We know what the dog was doing back then, and we have seen what it is doing now. They ask no more of their dogs today than they did in 1902. In true English tradition, they are still training the dogs as their grandfathers did. We in America have taken our dog light-years ahead using a lot of scientific information about learning. In actual work our young dogs, not far from being just puppies, are required to do more work than finished dogs in Britain. So, to my eye, tradition has held back that part of their sport.

But the British cannot be written off that easily. They have made a major contribution to the world of the hunting retriever. Without the British we wouldn't have retrievers today.

3

Where Did They Come From?

We in America may not be very appreciative of the way our British cousins train or use their retrievers, but there is no doubt that without the English we never would have had the great retrievers that we have today. Oh, yes, the Scots and the Irish got into the act too.

Today we think of our retrievers in terms of individual breeds with pure bloodlines and impeccable pedigrees. The oldest English retriever that is still around is the Curly-Coated. The best known are the Labrador, the Golden, the Flat-Coated, and the Irish Water Spaniel. The Chessie, although not English, as we have already seen, stems from the predecessor of the Labrador. As we will soon see, even the American Water Spaniel was "made" from English stock. Along the way came the English Water Spaniel, the Wavy-Coated Retriever, the Portland Dog, the Rough Water Dog, and a whole host of retrieving dogs who have been lost in time and many whose origins were not English—the Poodle, for one, though it is not much of a hunter these days.

THE RETRIEVER.

Originally the retriever was not a breed of dog but simply any dog that retrieved.

Retrievers at First Were Nondescript

If this treatise had been written two hundred years ago, the term *retrieving dog* would have referred to the kind of work the dog did, not to any special breed. Size, shape, or color had little to do with the designation. If a dog would retrieve a stick, it had potential; and if it liked feathers and brought back birds, it was a retriever.

One has to understand those times to try to fathom where our retrievers came from. Travel and communications were cumbersome at best, and in the confined world of the dog writer there was little real information to go on. Hearsay and supposition were his best tools. When this writer unlocked the history of the Labrador Retriever,* it soon became evident that the

*R. A. Wolters, *The Labrador Retriever . . . The History . . . The People* (Los Angeles: Petersen Publishing Co., 1981).

writers of the nineteenth century knew more about the dogs than they did about the dogs' history. And by the time they had repeated the inaccurate stories their predecessors had written, their stories had become a jumbled mass of misinformation. The writers failed to do their homework. Here is an example of what that means.

Hawker's Book— a Milestone

Lieutenant Colonel Peter Hawker, in his book *Instructions to a Young Sportsman,* first published in 1814, was the first writer to mention the dog that became the Labrador in England. Authors who followed merely copied Hawker with a little embroidery of their own. They could not even seem to get the dates correct. Somehow the year 1830 became associated with Hawker's book. (Actually 1830 was the year of the popular book's second edition.) So it is easy for a researcher today to see which writers merely copied their predecessors. If the writer uses the 1830 date, you know he did not go back to the original but used the material someone else had written. For a hundred years writers simply copied one another without ever understanding how the Labrador came about or how it was used. To this day writers are still claiming the Newfoundland Water Dog (one of the names used before Labrador was accepted)* was a descendant of the big Newfoundland, and its job was to swim the net lines in the cold fishing waters of the Grand Banks. A little research will show that, as we have already seen, the fishermen never used nets. And more research will show that the "descendant" was actually the original dog; the true story is just the reverse of what these writers say.

The year 1814 actually becomes a very important clue to unraveling the story that Hawker himself never tried to figure out. If 1830 is used, the accepted story won't work with history. Here is why: Hawker wrote, "Poole [Harbor] was, till of late years, the best place to buy Newfoundland dogs; either just imported, or broke in: but now they are become much more

---

*"Newfoundland dog," "Small Newfoundland," "Lesser Newfoundland," "St. John's dog," and "Water Dog" were all names used until about 1870, when the name "Labrador" came into general use.

scarce, owing (the sailors observe) to the strictness of 'those ——— tax
gatherers.' "

The key in that sentence is "till of late years," meaning from about 1800
to 1814. For almost 175 years writers have read that phrase and passed it over.
(Hawker's book has never been out of print.) The writers thought the
Labradors became scarce because of the import duty put on the dog. Possibly
Hawker believed that, too, since he did imply it. But the thing that Hawker
and all the dog writers that followed did not know was that Lord Malmesbury, who lived near Poole, started buying the dogs from Newfoundland at
the turn of the nineteenth century. A full kennel of them was kept pure
throughout his lifetime and on until his son's death in 1889. Certainly a small
tax on the dog was not going to deter aristocrats and hunters, who were
gentlemen of means, from buying this dog from Newfoundland. Hawker
should have realized that and not taken the sailors' reason as fact.

If Hawker didn't think of it back in his day, a good researcher should
have in the intervening years. The question remained. The dogs did become
scarce in Poole by 1814, and practically nonexistent there by 1830. Why?

The entrance to the stable at Heron Court, where Lord Malmesbury housed his
kennel of Labradors. *(Courtesy of the Earl of Malmesbury)*

The Answer Lies
in Poole's Economy

The port of Poole, because of the fishing trade that started in 1498, a year after John Cabot discovered Newfoundland, became one of the wealthiest economic centers in England. For 250 years, Newfoundland was completely controlled by business cartels in London, Poole, and Bristol, with the complete protection of the British fleet. But because of a long series of social and economic changes in Newfoundland, which took effect and became a major factor about 1750 when the fleet lost control, the British stranglehold on the island was ended. It took about forty years for the effect to be complete. Newfoundlanders took over the fishing business themselves and cut the English out. So in 1790 the English fishing fleet changed its main business and, instead of fishing, sailed to Labrador, where the seal hunting industry had started. By 1814 only a trickle of the fishing trade with New-foundland was left.

When Hawker wrote in that year that Poole had been the best place to get the dog from Newfoundland, but of late the dog was hard to come by, he most likely did not realize that the ten-thousand-man fishing fleet was no longer going from Poole to Newfoundland each year to fish for cod, but to Labrador to hunt seal. The dog was "hard to come by" not because of a tax but because few vessels were plying back and forth to Newfoundland. As we shall see later, moreover, because of certain laws there were fewer dogs in Newfoundland to bring back to England.

Piecing together the story of a breed of dog by using historical records is a technique that will not work as well for the other retriever breeds. Only in the case of the Labrador does written history show us where a dog came from and how it was developed. The stories of all the other retrievers, dogs deliberately bred into what they are, are a big question mark because the main sources for them are those same nineteenth-century dog writers who just didn't have the means—or do the research—for accurate reporting.

Poole became a flourishing city as great wealth was amassed from the fishing industry and mansions like the one in the old engraving below were built. *(Author Photos)*

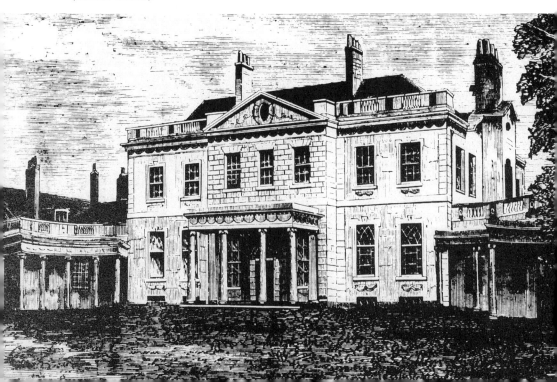

The Big Newfoundland Dog's Mistaken Credit

Let us use more of the documented reporting on the Labrador to explode a false theory about the beginnings of all the retrievers. Hawker calls the imported dog a "proper Labrador" and a "St. John's dog." Over the next fifty years, the dog goes by many other names, Smaller Newfoundland, Water Dog, and Lesser Newfoundland. At times the situation becomes confused because the large dog, what we call the Newfoundland today, was well known in Britain before the smaller dog came on the scene at the beginning of the nineteenth century. The big Newfoundland became the darling of the aristocratic estates, the playmate and protector of children. Psychologically, it just seemed correct, to those dog people in the early nineteenth century, that the big dog, which was already known in England, was the source for the new, smaller dog, who was also a strong swimmer.

This assumption just seemed to appear in the literature. The names "Smaller Newfoundland" and "Lesser Newfoundland" somehow took on a new meaning. The word *lesser* no longer simply meant "smaller," but was taken as implying that the smaller dog was a subvariety evolved from the larger animal. Possibly Hawker set the stage for this error by implying that the St. John's dog was a variety of the Newfoundland dog.

Taking advantage of that word, *lesser,* the Newfoundland writers claimed and still claim that their big dog is the "Mother lode," the breed from which all retrievers are descended. In Margaret Chern's book *The New Complete Newfoundland* (1975) is a chapter titled "The Great Newfoundland Family." In this chapter Ms. Chern gives credit to the "Newfoundland proper," as she refers to the big dog, for the Labrador, Chesapeake, Golden, Curly-Coated and Flat-Coated retrievers. The mistaken assumption on which this credit was based is that the St. John's dog was a "lesser" Newfoundland, bred down from the big dog. Chern claims that Newfoundland genes are in all these dogs. All those breeds of dogs from a Mother lode that can't hunt and has no nose for game?

If Chern had consulted more history instead of relying on the inaccurate guesswork of the dog writers before her time, she would have realized that Newfoundland, the island, was in a unique situation in the New World. It was not a colony of the Crown: in fact, just the opposite. The Crown used the British Navy to keep people from living on Newfoundland. The law stated that no building could be built with a chimney, in order to prevent people from living there over the harsh winter. Newfoundland was a fishing station owned and operated out of Poole by British money interests. The businessmen knew that if Newfoundland was settled, colonists would take over the lucrative commercial fishing industry and cut the British interests out. A deal that lasted over two hundred years was made between the money interests and the Crown. It involved the ten thousand fishermen who went to Avalon on the southeast coast of Newfoundland each spring to fish and returned to Poole each fall. If the Crown protected the industry by not allowing ship jumping and settlements to spring up, the Crown in times of war could use the fishermen, who were expert seamen, in the Royal Navy. As late as 1800 the navy hanged ship jumpers from their yardarms, but by then it was too late—settlements were well entrenched.

There was one exception to the ban on people living over the winter on the island, and this is where our hero, the dog, comes into the act. Within five years of the discovery of Newfoundland, France, Portugal, and Spain (especially the Basques) joined England in fishing the most productive waters in the world: the banks. Cabot reported that if he lowered a bucket into the water fish would be in it when it was drawn up. Each country fished in its own area, and there were enough fish so that no war was ever waged over the fishing rights, though the French navy did harass the fishing fleets from time to time. France had a settlement on the southern coast of the island. But the British squadron was always close at hand. This, as we shall see, becomes important in the development of the big Newfoundland dog.

Important for our retrievers, the English were the only ones who did shore fishing. They worked from the beaches, whereas the men from other countries lived on their vessels and fished from them. The British built workrooms and drying sheds. The records at Poole show that they worked in teams of four: two men fished from a small dory and two men prepared the catch. The fishing is still done the same way in Newfoundland today.

In October when the fleet returned to England, there was an important job still to be done in Newfoundland. Over the winter the sheds, workrooms, and dories had to be repaired and made ready for the next season.

Early eighteenth-century drawing of the British worksheds for the fishing industry in Newfoundland.

Men from Devon, the finest woodsmen in England, as mentioned in Chapter 1, were recruited for this job. They were experts at hunting and eking out a living in their forests in the west of England and were skilled craftsmen. They were sent over to Newfoundland to serve as winter work crews and were the exception to the ban on people living on the island over the winter. But even they were rotated each year so that they would not try to settle on Avalon.

Newfoundland in those days was a harsh no-man's-land where hanging, flogging, and murder were the regular way of life. Ship jumping from the fishing fleet was a serious offense and meant death if one were caught, but even so this didn't deter many who couldn't take the harsh life. Newfoundland was tough country for a deserter to live in. It became the haven for the most notorious pirates in history. Henry Mainwarring, feared throughout the Spanish world, described Newfoundland as the best of all places to recruit a fighting crew. There were no civilized institutions: no church, no formal law, no courts, no schools, no business enterprises, no roads—it was a bleak place.

The work crews from Devon had to do their repair work and also manage to survive. As there was no indigenous dog on the island, they took

Of blacke hounds aunciently come from
Sainct Huberts abbay in Ar-
dene.   Chap. 5

An important woodcut from *The Book of Hunting* by George Turberville, 1576.
The black dog bears a good likeness to today's Labrador.

with them their hunting dog from home. It was called the St. Huberts dog,
a dog we know they had because it is recorded in *The Book of Hunting,* an
Elizabethan manuscript written in 1576 by George Turberville. A later text
states:

> The dogs are commonly all black, yet nevertheless, their race is so mingled
> these days, that we find them of all colors. This kind of dog is mighty of body,
> nevertheless their legs are low and short, likewise they are not swift, although
> they be very good of scent, hunting chases for tracking wounded game. The
> dog fearing neither water or cold and do more covet the chase that smells, they
> find themselves neither of swiftness nor courage to hunt and kill. The dogs
> of this color prove good, especially those that are coal black. Yet I once found
> a book which a hunter dedicated to the Prince of Lorayne, wherein was a
> rhyme about a dog called Soygllard who was white.

> My name came first from holy Huberts Race
> Soygllard my sir, a dog of singular grace

> Whereupon we may presume that some of the kind prove white, whereupon
> but they are not the kind we have at these days.

One of the displays at the Poole museum showing artifacts from Newfoundland *(Author Photo)*

This is a good description of our Lab today.* He is not a hunter or a killer. He likes the water and can stand the cold. Most are black, but the recessive yellow gene is discussed at this early date. We will talk about that later.

The St. Huberts dog was introduced into England from France. The old woodcut illustration from Turberville's book shows it to be as close to today's Lab as you can get.

The dog became the work crews' meal ticket. He hunted on land and water. When the men went back home, the dog stayed on and worked for the fishermen. It was soon discovered that he was so fantastic in the water that he was used in the fishing dories.

This is documented in the Poole museum and in a seaman's journal written in 1794 on board HMS *Boston.* "The Fishermen, when they hooked a Fish, in drawing the line up find the fish sometimes disentangled themselves. The Fish may sometimes float on the water. The Dog, observing this, dasheth into the Sea and brings the Fish alongside."

*The St. Huberts dog theory is the result of research done in 1980 with the help of Stephen Ferguson, curator of rare books, Firestone Library, Princeton University. Later in the course of research in England, it was discovered that Lorna Countess Howe came to the same conclusion in 1957.

A Few Questions and Some Practical Answers

The first question to ask the Newfoundland dog writers who still think their dog was the original dog on the island is: Why would the original work crews from Devon take a dog with them who could not hunt? Remember, this was a tough society and every mouth had to earn its own keep. Then ask, Why would the fishermen in a small dory take along a 180-pound dog that had

A Newfoundland dog is almost three times the size of the Labrador. No way could it be used to retrieve fish in and out of a two-man dory. *(Author Photo)*

long hair? Try getting such a dog in and out of a small boat without swamping it!

For practical reasons the nonhunting big dog could not have been the original dog and the smaller dog have been bred down from it. Now let's let history prove the point that the smaller St. Huberts dog was the first dog, and after 1713 the bigger Newfoundland dog was bred up to make an animal that would serve as a dray dog.

We have already said that there was no indigenous dog. To establish our facts we have to make that point very clear: there was no dog on the island when the British started their fishing. The Newfoundland dog writers try to claim there was.

Cabot in his journals never mentions a dog. Lieutenant John Cartwright, in his journals in the U.S. Library of Congress, shows that there was no dog on the island. Cartwright in the mid-1700s describes the Beothuk Indians, the only natives on Newfoundland. They were a sorry society who had been banished to the island by the mainland Indians. Cartwright writes, "To complete their wretched condition Providence has even denied them the pleasing services and companionship of a faithful dog." His brother, Captain George Cartwright, wrote that they were the most forlorn of any of the human species except for the Indians of Tierra del Fuego, and "not even possessed of the useful services of a dog." In their journals the Cartwrights made a drawing to show how the Indians hunted deer without dogs.

Not to belabor the point, but the Dorset Indians had lived for a short time on the north end of the island. Although their race disappeared two hundred years before the white man appeared, they too had no dog and pulled their sleds themselves. Five hundred years before Cabot, the Vikings landed on Newfoundland. That settlement has been discovered but no archaeological find has ever been made anywhere on Newfoundland that shows that any dog was there. The Newfoundland dog people claim the Algonquin and Sioux Indians had a big dog that the British settlers found and called the Newfoundland. The Algonquin and Sioux Indians were never near Newfoundland! And if the writers understood the history of this fishing station, they would have realized that there were no British settlers until 250 years after the fishing industry started. And nowhere could I find such a British settler's quote as they claim.

The Newfoundland dog writers use part of the facts in some of their material to prove their dog was indigenous to the island. Their "proof" is

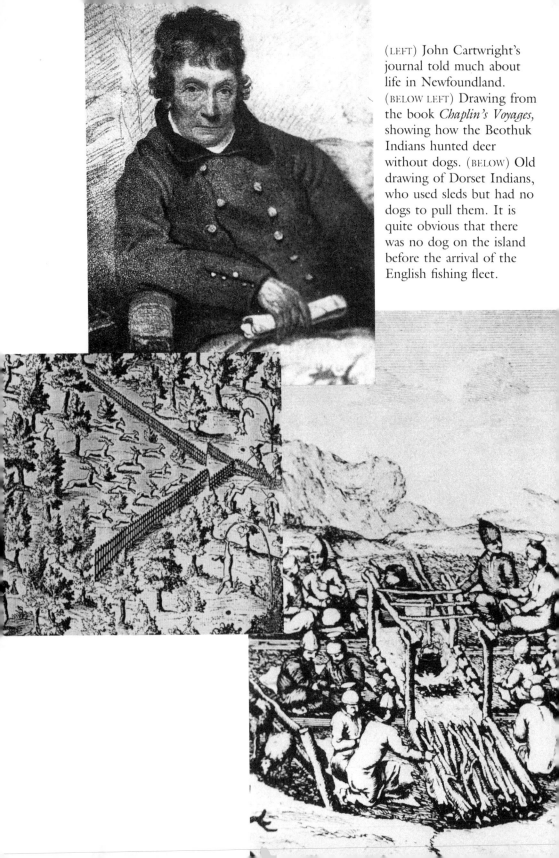

(LEFT) John Cartwright's journal told much about life in Newfoundland. (BELOW LEFT) Drawing from the book *Chaplin's Voyages*, showing how the Beothuk Indians hunted deer without dogs. (BELOW) Old drawing of Dorset Indians, who used sleds but had no dogs to pull them. It is quite obvious that there was no dog on the island before the arrival of the English fishing fleet.

that McCormack, the first explorer to cross the island, met Indians with a large black dog. There is no question that this was true. But here are the facts. The Indians he encountered were of the Micmac tribe from Nova Scotia, and, true, the dog they had was the big Newfoundland dog. The dog writers do not report that McCormack made his island crossing in 1822. That's three hundred years after the whole dog story began. The last of the indigenous Indians, a Beothuk woman, died in St. John's in 1829. By the date of McCormack's crossing of the island, the Water Dog, the early Lab, was already in England and his story had been told in print. Generations of the dog had already been produced in the Malmesbury kennel at Poole; Hawker had already written his book, and the big Newfoundland dog had been on the British estates for over half a century taking care of the children and scaring off poachers. McCormack's exploration and findings were too late to mean much in the story of the Newfoundland dog or Lab.

So how did the big dog get there? This was a tough part of the world and an animal or man had to have a compelling reason to exist there. The treaty of Utrecht in 1713 started the socioeconomic change in Newfoundland. It put the French off the island. When the British fleet consequently stopped its close surveillance of the Newfoundland coast after 1713, ship jumpers started living along the coast, in coves where the fleet could not easily get to them. The numbers grew steadily. By 1750 the settlers were starting their own fishing industry, and by 1787, according to the journal of seaman Aaron Thomas, the population of St. John's was 19,106, of whom 5,338 were children, so we know that family life was in progress. Life was rugged, and one problem was that there was no wood for fires near at hand. Here was a job for a big dog, as there were no horses on the island. If you needed a large dog, where would you get it? I shall leave it to the Newfoundland dog writers to decide which dog (the St. Bernard, the Mastiff, or something else?) was used to breed up the existing Water Dog to a size that would permit it to drag logs eight miles to the fireplaces in St. John's.

The big dogs retained the swimming ability of the Water Dog but lost the hunting instinct. They were taught to work in a harness and drag a log on the snow, unattended, from the woods to town and return for another log. They were so successful at it that these dogs were brought to Poole Harbor, and dog-cart trains were run between there and London until it was considered too cruel and stopped. That is the story of the Newfoundland dog. I hope this will put an end to their claim that their dog was the basic stock for our hunting retrievers.

To Get the Facts, Dog Writers Didn't Help

As we have said in Chapter 1, the British were the best of breeders. The British Isles have produced the best milk cows the world has seen, and their horses are the finest. When it came to dogs, they again were masters.

There were no public records of animal breeding. The Kennel Club didn't come into existence until 1873. It may not be fair to blame the early writers for the inadequate records. There were such class distinctions at that time that writers did not have the status to associate with the aristocracy on whose large estates the breeding programs took place. Here is a perfect example: Hawker knew Poole harbor, in that day one of the finest duck-hunting areas in England, but never knew that the second earl of Malmesbury, who was the undersecretary of foreign affairs under Lord Canning, kept kennels of hunting Labradors at Heron Court, only four miles from Poole, where Hawker hunted. The dogs were for the private hunting of the earl and his friends. The earl was an ardent hunter. Records in his game books, which cover forty years of hunting, list more than forty thousand birds shot over his dogs. His son, the third earl, foreign secretary under Disraeli, kept the kennels going until his death. The point is that two generations of earls kept the dogs pure, yet no dog writer ever saw them or wrote about them. The same thing happened in Scotland, where the dukes of Buccleuch and Lord Home also kept Labradors, but not a word can be found about them until almost the twentieth century. The dog writer never traveled in those circles.

This seems a fair observation as regards the early writers. Later in the century there was no excuse for the lack of important breeding facts in dog reporting.

The St. John's Dog

Through Hawker's writings, the St. John's dog was immediately recognized as a superior worker. At a time when there was no such thing in the hunters' kennels as a true retrieving breed of dog, except possibly the Poodle, the introduction of the Water Dog from Newfoundland provided the necessary genes to improve the retrieving work of dogs used for hunting. This cross-breeding was carried on for the next seventy-five years.

What actually happened to the dog is easy to understand. So few were brought in to Poole that if it hadn't been for the Malmesbury line the dogs would have disappeared. Those that did get in and were bought by hunters were bred to whatever cross suited their owners. Except for the Heron Court dogs, that original line, the St. John's Water Dog, was lost by the hunters' haphazard breeding programs.

Retrievers Go Back into Antiquity

The retriever was not a new phenomenon at the time of its introduction from the New World. Excerpts from as far back as Gervase Markham's book *The Art of Fowling by Water and Land* (1621) tell us:

> The water dogge is a creature of such generall use, and so frequent in use amongst us heere in England, that it is needless to make an large description of him: the rather since not any amongst us is so simple that he cannot say when hee seeth him. . . . Your dogge may be of any color and yet excellent, and his hair in generall would be long and curled, not loose and shagged.

. . . Now for the cutting or shaving him from the Navill downward, or backward, it is two wayes well to be allowed of this, for summer hunting or for the water; because these Water Dogges naturally are ever most laden with hairs on the hind parts, nature as it were labouring to defend that part most. The hinder parts are ever deeper in the water than the fore parts, therefore nature has given the great armour of haire to defent the wette and coldnesse; yet this defence in the Sommer time by the violence of the heate of the Sunne, and the greatness of the Dogges labor is very noysome and troublesome, and maketh him sooner to faint and give over his sport.

The Poodle??

We must assume that this "dogge" sometimes referred to as a Rough Water Dog is a "mixed-up Poodle." Reading all the dog writers, starting fifty years before Markham with Dr. Caius (who calls it a Water Spaniel or finder), one will find their descriptions somewhat confusing, but they do add up to a Poodle of some kind. In 1780 Reidel calls it a *Pudel*. Taplin in 1803 has it looking like a Bearded Collie, Old English Sheepdog, and an Otter Hound mix. Bingley believes it came from Spain. Thomas Bell writes that the dog should not be confused with the Water Spaniel. The "great authority" Mr. John H. Walsh, who used the pseudonym Stonehenge, wrote in 1859 that the Poodle was probably the original Water Spaniel. Take your pick!

Poodles are one of the oldest breeds. They may have been the dog carved on Roman tombs around A.D. 30 and on coins. They appear in the writings of Konrad von Gesner in 1553 and in fifteenth-century paintings from France, Holland, and Italy. They existed in Russia, Germany, and France. The Germans are given credit for developing the dog as we know it. They called them "Pudels," and the dogs were taken to Holland, where they were known as "Poedels." It's believed the Germans introduced them into France, where they developed a working dog of medium-size called the

This drawing is over four hundred years old. It was published in *The Sketch Book of Jean de Tournes,* in Lyons, France, 1556. This is the Rough Water Dog going after a downed duck. It establishes that retrieving dogs were used in mid-sixteenth-century France.

"Caniche." The Poodle became a great favorite and was taken from the duck blind into the boudoir.

When the dog entered England is anyone's guess, but it was most likely brought in by the waterfowlers of the eastern and southern coasts. It became known in England as the Rough Water Dog. Dr. Johannes Caius, physician to Queen Elizabeth I, included the Poodle in his book *De Canibus Britannicis* in 1570.

My guess is that the Rough Water Dog, or Poodle, got into a lot of the mixes of early retrievers. It seems possible that this dog got into the Irish Water Spaniel; especially if Nick Waters's "Asia" theory is correct, as you will read next!

The Rough Water Dog seems to be a variety of the Poodle. This comes from *The Sportsman's Cabinet* by Taplin, 1803.

The Irish Water Spaniel—Ancient or Modern?

Searching for the origins of the Irish Water Spaniel is much the same as looking for those of the other retrievers. In some ways, the answers to the questions on its past were right at the end of the noses of the writers of the period, but they couldn't see them.

An Irish law enacted in A.D. 17 specifically refers to an Irish Spaniel. The history of the breed as we know it, however, perhaps begins with Mr. Justin M. McCarthy of Dublin, who had a kennel of the Irish for some fifteen years

The Irish Water Spaniel has a lot in common with the Rough Water Dog and the Poodle. *(A. H. Rowan, Jr., Photo)*

in the 1830s and 1840s. His dog Boatswain seems to have been the "father" of the breed. Boatswain was born in 1834 and was put down, according to a letter McCarthy wrote in *The Field*, in 1849. In his letter he said the dog was eighteen years old; the dates only count up to fifteen. Maybe McCarthy was better at dog breeding than mathematics. The important thing is that the date does set the time when the Irish Water Spaniel was used in the shooting sports.

The sad part about it is that the earliest reference to the Irish Water Spaniel seems to be in a book called *Dogs: Their Origin and Varieties,* written by H. D. Richardson in 1847. This book was published in Dublin and was the first major dog book printed in Ireland. Note the year. It was published while McCarthy had his kennel, which he abandoned in 1849 to spend some time abroad in France. Richardson describes the Irish Water Spaniel in every detail—even to the tuft or topknot. He calls it a "genuine water-spaniel." Richardson and McCarthy were in the same city at the same time, and Richardson wrote a book on the origins of dogs and still did not get the story of the origins of the Irish Water Spaniel. It was not that McCarthy, who might have enlightened Richardson, was not well known for his Irish dogs. As McCarthy himself wrote, Boatswain and his son Jack, owned by Jolliffe Tuffnell of Merrion Square, Dublin, "were known particularly as sires to everyone in Ireland, and to very many in England." McCarthy dogs, he insisted, always sold for a very high price.

McCarthy does not say in his writings where he obtained the dog or how he bred it. This much he does say: "They will not stand a cross with any other breed: the spaniel, setter, Newfoundland dog, and Labrador dog, &c., perfectly destroy coat, ears, tail and symmetry; added to which, the cross-breed dog is very difficult to dry. I have bred with great care, giving the highest prices for good dogs to cross my own." Author Richardson, who was on the scene at the time, could have documented McCarthy's work in his book, but unfortunately he fails even to mention it.

A. E. Knox refers to the Irish Water Spaniel in his book *Game Birds and Wildfowl* (1850), and the first known painting of the Irish was done in 1841. The timing of this book supports the concept that the Irish Water Spaniel of the type we know today had not been in existence very long at that time.

Stonehenge, in *The Dog in Health and Disease* (1895), only confuses the issue by declaring that there are two distinct varieties of the Irish. He too does not get to the heart of the matter. Boatswain and McCarthy are generally accepted as the "father figures" of the breed, but the question is did McCarthy save an old breed from extinction or "manufacture" a new breed by careful selection and what he referred to as "giving the highest prices for good dogs to cross my own"?

What could the old breed be that McCarthy could have saved? Nick Waters, in his book *A Bundle of Rags in a Cyclone (The Irish Water Spaniel)* (Rodington, Shropshire, n.d.), makes a most interesting observation:

> Countries of the Near and Middle East were in a comparatively advanced state of civilization long before Ireland, and it is conceivable that traders from these countries should visit Ireland, as they did other countries, taking with them their dogs, as do travellers today. Looking at photographs of Afghan Hounds, of sixty or seventy years ago, one notices many similarities with the Irish Water Spaniel, a smooth face, hair on the top of the head growing to a point between the eyes, fore legs feathered all the way around, often with a smooth patch just above the foot, hind legs also well coated often with a smooth patch in front, between the hock and the foot. The coat is also shorter on the body than on the legs.

Waters raises the remote idea that there might be a distant relationship between the Afghan and the Irish, that both may share a remotely ancient common ancestor. Gradually over the years in Ireland, man has helped evolve the Irish Water Spaniel we know today. Could the Irish we know be the Afghan mixed with the Rough Water Dog, Britain's version of the Poodle?

Waters's observation could give the Irish Water Spaniel a much more romantic beginning than the story that McCarthy "manufactured" him. Add to that the fact that in Irish laws that go back, as we have seen, to the time of Christ (A.D. 17), specific mention is made of Irish Spaniels. That can start the imagination going.

Just a thought. The Afghan dog comes from Asia Minor. History does tell us that the Irish were conquered by Iberians who came by way of Spain. They had migrated there from Asia Minor. Later the Iberians were known as the Irish Celts. Another thought: probably the first or earliest written reference to a water dog is in a Persian manuscript of 4000 B.C. Right or not, thinking about it is fascinating.

Was the Curly-Coated Retriever First?

We know there once were breeds of retrievers called the British Water Spaniel, the English Water Spaniel, and the Tweed Water Spaniel, but they no longer exist. The Curly-Coated is supposedly the oldest of the retrievers that we still have today. It is thought that it stems from the English Water Spaniel of the sixteenth century. Once again we run into the old malady of all the writers copying from their predecessors. They all say the dog originated with the English Water Spaniel. They all say that dog had its origins in the sixteenth century. They say it was crossed with a retrieving setter (with no explanation of what that was). They say the Curly might have been a cross with the Irish Water Spaniel. If this is so, then the Irish is older than the Curly. However, they also say that instead of the Irish it might have been the Rough Water Dog, a sort of Poodle. So the story is a confusing one for us today. All are also very sure the St. John's dog was added to the mix, and some believe that in the late 1880s the Poodle was bred back into the Irish breed to "tighten" its curl. Some conjecture that it was this mix (Irish and Poodle) that was one of the crosses in our Chesapeake Bay Retriever.

Eileen Clarke's statement in her book *How to Raise and Train Curly-Coated Retrievers* (1966) that the Curly was recognized as a breed by the Kennel Club in 1854 is obviously an error: the Kennel Club was not founded until 1873.

The Curly was one of the most popular of all the retrievers in the late nineteenth century, but like women's fashions, without any explanation, the dog practically disappeared. It was replaced by the Wavy-Coated Retriever. None of the professional dog writers of the day seems to have left any record of why it happened. The writers of the day wrote almost nothing about the actual field work of these dogs.

The answer seems to be found not in the professional writings of the day but in a note to the editor published in the April 1880 *Kennel Gazette:* "Curley retrievers have, no doubt, fallen off as a class, not only in quantity but in quality. This may be easily accounted for by the proportionate rise in the public estimation of their Wavy Coat cousins. The latter are generally supposed to be better workers, less headstrong, and therefore easier broken, and also far less inclined to be hard in the mouth; and I may also add that I have undoubtedly found Wavy retrievers the better-tempered of the two."

The Curly-Coated Retriever has an excellent, hard, tight coat for hunting.
(Alan Coman Photo)

Wavy-Coated Retrievers

Stonehenge, in *The Dog,* writes in 1887 of the Wavy-Coated: "This fashionable breed now considered a necessary adjunct to every shooter, is often pure St. John or Labrador; at other times it is more or less crossed with a setter." Reread his statement and you too may get the feeling that the author is not sure of himself.

Although the term *Wavy-Coated Retriever* remained in common use till the end of the nineteenth century, it gradually was replaced with the *Flat-Coated Retriever* as the fashion changed. Despite what Stonehenge wrote, there was little or no chance of pure Water Dogs (St. John's dog or Labradors still coming from Newfoundland as late as 1887. By that time the dog trade in Poole was over). A cross with the Collie and/or the setter seems very likely. In any case, a long-haired Labrador at that time would have been a mix, not pure.

There Is Another "Puzzlement"

With the advent of the Flat-Coated Retriever, once again a responsible breeder is identified as having developed a breed. S. E. Shirley in 1873, at age twenty-nine, founded the Kennel Club in England and was its chairman and president for twenty-five years. One can say without a doubt that through his efforts the Wavy-Coated Retriever was transformed into the Flat-Coated with consistent repeatable results. The "puzzlement" is: Why didn't Stonehenge, the most important writer of the day, get the information about the Flat- and the Wavy-Coated retrievers from the expert, a man everyone knew, the president of the Kennel Club?

The Flat-Coated Retriever has a softer coat than a Labrador and is not so easy to train. (*A. H. Rowan, Jr., Photo*)

Before 1850 Shirley's father already had kennels of fine Curly- and Wavy-Coated retrievers. The Shirleys had plenty of stock to work from. The head of the early Wavy-Coated had an almost straight line between the skull and the nose, which indicated a Collie influence. S. E. Shirley changed that in the Flat-Coated dog by giving it a broader head with more of a *stop* (the step up from the muzzle to the skull). Though it was a handsome dog and a good worker, the Flat-Coated did not stay in vogue very long.

The Golden Comes on the Scene

Where did this fellow come from? The story started in 1860, and it is a very colorful one. For the first time, it seems as if we have a lot of detail about the origin of a new retriever—only to have our hopes dashed! At first this dog went by several different names. He was called the Russian Tracker, Yellow Russian Retriever, Yellow Retriever, Flat-Coated Golden Retriever, and finally Golden Retriever.

To start looking into the dog's past, *The Golden Retriever Year Book* of 1939 tells this tale:

> There probably is less doubt concerning the origin of the Golden Retriever than there is concerning that of many breeds. This sporting breed, in the form we know it today, dates back to 1860, for it was in that year Sir Dudley Marjoribanks visited a circus at Brighton, England, and saw the immediate ancestors of the Golden.
>
> The circus was featuring a troupe of Russian performing dogs that were doing a rather elaborate routine under the direction of their Russian trainer. The feats accomplished by the dogs impressed Sir Dudley, and after the show he made an effort to purchase a pair of them. He reasoned that the intelligence evidenced in performing could be put to great use in the field.
>
> The Russian trainer, however, proved a problem. He refused to sell a pair on the grounds it would ruin his act. Perhaps it is just as well that he refused, for Sir Dudley—who was later to become the first Lord Tweedmouth—countered by making an offer for the entire troupe of eight dogs. The deal was accomplished.

The same story can be read in twenty or more other books and publications. The *American Kennel Gazette* tells it with a little more flair. They describe how Sir Dudley, during a jaunt to Brighton, southern England's famous recreational mecca, succumbed to the enticement of a barker and

The Golden Retriever has a mixed-up story, but it turned out handsome. *(A. H. Rowan, Jr., Photo)*

bought a ticket to the circus. As soon as he took his seat, a dog act came on that caught his full attention. The eight big taffy-colored fellows were so huge that they seemed clumsy, but they complied readily with the commands barked out by the Russian trainer. Sir Dudley saw that the dogs were not only agile but extremely intelligent as well.

As soon as the act was over, Sir Dudley "made a beeline" for the stage door (as the *Gazette* relates). Then its story is much the same as all the rest. Soon the dogs were on their way from Brighton to Sir Dudley's estate in the Guisachan deer forest in Inverness-shire, Scotland. None of the accounts mentions how much he paid for the dogs, or how he shipped them that distance.

Sir Dudley is alleged to have bred the eight dogs for ten years without resorting to any outside cross. At the end of that time he was ready, but he "threw up his hands" (most of the accounts mention this) because Scotland did not offer any game suitable to the dogs' size. They weighed one hundred pounds and stood thirty inches high. Reading this, one wonders why he didn't try them on the famous Scottish stag.

The *Gazette* continues:

> Then one day he found the same answer that proved successful with other new breeds . . . a cross with the Bloodhound. Whether this was suggested to him or just an inspiration has never been recorded. The cross, which he only did once, eliminated all the faults he had discovered in the Russian Tracker. First, of course, it intensified the scenting power, then it brought about a reduction in size, caused a refinement in the texture of the coat and darkened the latter.

Now the True Story

It is hard to say when that story was first written. According to these accounts, the dogs were bought in 1860 and bred to the Bloodhound in 1870. Then, as the story goes, the dog had immediate success. That story lasted some sixty or more years until it was proved to be only the figment of someone's imagination. Discovered in 1952, the original stud book written in Lord Tweedmouth's hand covering the period from 1835 to 1890 gave a detailed account of the breeding operation at Guisachan. There was no mention of any Russian circus dogs, no mention of the transportation of eight dogs—information that would have been expected of as careful a recordkeeper as Tweedmouth.

The fiction writers who concocted that "fairy tale" must have giggled all the way to their graves. The "succumbing to the enticements of the barker" at the circus; "it was the first act as he sat down"; "he beelined to the stage door"; "the haggling over two or eight dogs"—to write that fiction and pass it off as fact takes skill and imagination even for a twisted mind.

Once again I point out that there were many strange men of the dog-writing profession during this period. Here was a successful dog and all knew where to get them, yet no one took the time to get the story from the mouth of Tweedmouth. So we have just another example of the trail of misinformation that the nineteenth-century dog writers left as their legacy.

There have been only two writers that I could find who even questioned the Golden story. The first was the British writer and dog judge A. Croxton-Smith, who wrote in *Country Life* magazine in the late 1920s (as reported in the *American Kennel Gazette*), "The origin of the breed was unknown and . . . to say the Golden Retriever was a Russian Retriever was to repeat a myth." This is all he wrote about it, yet this information came to Croxton-Smith in 1927 from the third Lord Tweedmouth, who claimed to know where and from whom his grandfather had bought his first yellow retriever. If Croxton-Smith had followed through and asked what the grandson knew, it might have led to more than his just questioning the circus story. The grandson named person and place, but Smith did nothing about it. This information was not made public for another twenty-five years.

The American dog writer William F. Brown, in his book *Retriever Gun Dogs* (1945), tells the "fairy tale" about the circus dogs, then goes on to say that he does not want to doubt this official version of the Golden Retriever Club. He points out, however, that in the early days, what was designated as the "Russian Retriever" was not held in high esteem by the British sporting fraternity. The breed was considered too cumbersome, the coat undesirable for the shooting coverts. He goes on to guess correctly that the Golden breed stems from a Wavy-Coated or Flat-Coated Retriever "sport." *Sport* is the appropriate term for the occasional yellow or golden puppy that appeared in black litters in early years. This also happened in the early Labrador litters. It was a good guess on Brown's part.

Finally the Golden's Story

The precise records that Lord Tweedmouth left (they were found and reported in 1952) show a purchase in 1865 of a yellow retriever named Nous from a cobbler in Brighton. The dog had been given to the cobbler in payment of a debt and was the only yellow in an unregistered litter of black

Scottish keepers and handlers on the Guisachan estate about 1865. The dog on the left is Nous, who was the foundation on which Lord Tweedmouth "built" the Golden Retriever.

Wavy-Coated Retrievers. (That much of the story Lord Tweedmouth's grandson told to writer Croxton-Smith in 1927.)

Nous was bred in 1868 to Belle, a Tweed Water Spaniel that had been presented to Lord Tweedmouth by his cousin, David Robertson, from Ladykirk on the Tweed River. Four yellow bitches resulted. One of the puppies was given to the earl of Ilchester, and from this bitch and a mixture of Labradors and Wavy-Coated Retrievers a strain was developed called Melbury. The other three progeny were used, and for the next twenty years Lord Tweedmouth line-bred, an unusual plan for those days. He introduced the Tweed Water Spaniel into the "mix" again and then added two Wavy-Coateds to keep the strong hunting instincts in the line. Then an Irish Setter was brought in to improve the upland hunting ability and ensure color. Later a sandy-colored Bloodhound was used to improve the tracking ability. Result: the Golden Retriever that was bred and worked at Guisachan until 1905, when the estate was sold. It may not be as exciting a story as the Lab's, but at last that is the truth about the Golden Retriever.

In 1904 the International Gun Dog League's open stake was won by a liver Flat-Coated that was one of Lord Tweedmouth's breeding. Goldens were registered as Flat-Coated Retrievers (Golden) until 1913, when they became known as Golden or Yellow Retrievers. In 1920 the name Golden Retriever was accepted by the Kennel Club.

Where Was the Lab All This Time?

The last part of the nineteenth century becomes an important chapter in the development of retrievers in Britain. The Labrador comes into its own and outstrips all the other retrieving breeds. Let's see how it came about.

The Flat-Coated Retriever, as we have seen, was developed from the Wavy-Coated and had a very short fling in popularity as a shooting dog. The Flat-Coated, we know, then lost its popularity to the Labrador, who started appearing publicly in the middle 1880s.

The Tweed Water Spaniels, an old breed, were the result of an early

At the end of the nineteenth century, the Labrador came into its own. In the field, its popularity has never been challenged. *(Author Photo)*

cross between a Rough Water Dog and a Land Spaniel. They were "liver-colored," which could have meant they were anything from brown to yellow. They were developed in the Tweed River area of Scotland.

The Tweed, famous for its salmon fishing, flows eastward in the border region with England. The Tweed Water Spaniels were most popular in this area, but in relatively few years the breed became extinct.

In the late nineteenth century, the Tweed region became central in the development of the Labrador Retriever. Is it just coincidence or could we attribute the demise of the Tweed Water Spaniel partly to the Labrador? This border region is the next place to pick up the Labrador's story.

As you will recall, the Labrador was being bought and bred pure, according to the private writings of the second earl of Malmesbury, from the earliest days of the dog's arrival at Poole. We can assume that this breeding at nearby Heron Court began in 1801, when the earl started the family game book records, which he kept for the next forty years. The first record of using the dog appears in the edited version of the family game book under the date December 28, 1809. (The original game book was lost in a fire. The version edited by F. G. Affalo was called *Half a Century of Sport in Hampshire.*) Heron Court was the only place in England where there was a concentration of the dogs, the only place where there were enough Labradors to keep the lines going without mixing it into extinction.

A Fluke Saved the Labrador

The Heron Court kennels continued, unknown to the dog writers or hunters, for two generations of earls of Malmesbury. But also unknown even to the Malmesburys, the Scottish fifth duke of Buccleuch and the tenth earl of Home, who lived at the family estate, The Hirsel, on the Tweed River in Scotland, had both started kennels of Labradors. They obtained their dogs from the port of Greenock on Scotland's west coast. As previously stated, the trade between Poole and Newfoundland was just about finished, but a small trade was continued with the Scottish port by a Captain Hawker. (That name, Hawker, appears again. Both men are associated with harbors where the dog came into the British Isles.) It is believed that the Buccleuch kennel was started about 1835.

Once again, little is known about those early years. We do have a letter, dated 1839 and written from Naples, in which the fifth duke of Buccleuch states that he and the tenth lord Home are on his yacht with their Labradors Moses and Drake.

During this long period, between the beginning of the nineteenth century to about the 1870s, there were other aristocratic families that also imported and owned Labradors. They were friends of either the Malmesburys, the Buccleuchs, or the Homeses. The dogs belonging to this small circle were "lost" in time or absorbed into the Malmesbury or Buccleuch line of Labs. Almost all of the other dogs that got into the British Isles from Newfoundland were cross-bred out of existence in order to enhance other lines of retrievers. It was the two kennels, Malmesbury's in southern England and Buccleuch's in southern Scotland, that carried the pure New-foundland Water Dog or St. John's dog, called by the earl of Malmesbury the Labrador dog, into the twentieth century.

This would not have happened, and the Labrador would have gone into extinction, except for a fluke happening, a chance meeting between the next generation of these aristocratic patrons of the Labrador, the sixth duke of Buccleuch and the twelfth earl of Home, with the third earl of Malmesbury. When I spoke many years later with the fourteenth earl of Home, Sir Alec Douglas-Home, he told me that he too recalled the facts of this meeting: the "sick aunt" story.

The year would have been in the early 1880s. The background of the story is that before this time something had happened at the Buccleuch kennel. It may have been disease or some other calamity; the exact details have been lost in time. As a result, the kennel was seriously reduced in size. The important chance meeting took place after the calamity, but the timing is not known or even important. The present duke of Buccleuch neither confirms nor denies the story. Their record, the kennel stud book, starts in 1882 with a dog named Ned out of Lord Malmesbury's Juno, sired by his dog Sweep; not much documentation is known before that.

The story is that the twelfth lord Home took his friend the duke of Buccleuch on a trip south to Bournemouth, the seaport next to Poole, on the pretext of seeing a sick aunt; actually they went there for some of the best duck shooting in England.

The Third Earl

There they met the third earl of Malmesbury, from Poole. The earl was an avid hunter, whether it was with his own Labradors at Heron Court or deerstalking in Scotland. Malmesbury played an important role in opening the Scottish deer forests to the sport of stalking.

After the defeat of Bonnie Prince Charlie in 1746, much of Scotland lay waste for one hundred years. But now the English bought and rented vast estates in Scotland for the purpose of hunting the stag. Building roads, manor houses, railroads and many other services for the English sportsman revived the economy. Stalking became the fashionable sport for the British aristocracy when in the 1840s Queen Victoria and Prince Albert made Scotland their second home. Scotland became the favored playground for the English aristocracy and those grown rich from the industrial revolution. Prince Albert was absolutely "wild" for deerstalking, even killing two deer through his dining-room window at Balmoral Castle.

The third earl of Malmesbury was a man of many parts, a statesman and hunter. There is a great painting of him in deerstalker's garb hanging at the present family home, Graywell Hill. The photograph on page 74 showing the earl with his Labrador resting his head on his lap has historical significance. Until it was found by the author, the earliest known photograph of a Labrador had been one taken in 1867 of Lord Home's dog Nell, born in 1856. This newly found photograph is a daguerreotype. It is one of a kind: there is no negative, the image is on silver on a copper plate. An appraisal of this image dates it as about 1850.

The Lab's Future Is Secured

The chance meeting of fellow hunters, the third earl of Malmesbury, the sixth duke of Buccleuch, and the twelfth lord Home, secured the Labrador's future. Malmesbury invited the two visitors from Scotland to hunt ducks with him and they accepted. Both Scotsmen expressed their astonishment at seeing at Heron Court the same black retriever that they had at home. The upshot of this meeting was that when the duke and lord returned to Scotland they brought with them six dogs that the earl of Malmesbury had given them to rejuvenate and restock the Buccleuch kennel.

Why did the earl of Malmesbury do this? He was getting up in years and was concerned about the future of his own kennel. His father had passed the kennels down to him, but his son was not interested in hunting or in the dogs. The gift was the earl's way of making sure the Labrador's lineage would

The third earl of Malmesbury with one of his Labradors resting its head on the earl's knee. This is the oldest known photograph of a Labrador, taken between 1850 and 1852. From a daguerreotype in the author's collection.

continue. The earl was correct. Five years after his death in 1889 the kennel at Heron Court was gone. If that chance meeting had not taken place, the Labrador would not have survived in the pure form that we know it. Elsewhere the dog had been cross-bred with everything that came down the pike and was being more and more diluted with each generation. It would have been all over for the Labrador with the death of the third earl in England and the calamity that hit the Buccleuch kennels in Scotland.

The six dogs the Buccleuch kennel received from Malmesbury are the foundation stock for the dogs that made it into the present century. From the beginning of the St. John's dog, as Hawker knew it, from the Malmesbury kennels to the Buccleuch kennels, the modern Labrador comes down to us.

The Original Stock
Is Gone

The Labrador became a great success from the moment it was introduced to the public at the end of the nineteenth century and early in the twentieth. The Golden survived the pressure the Lab put on this market, but the newly developed Flat-Coated and the other retriever breeds took a back seat to the rising star—and some disappeared.

The Lab, through this later period, had two important patrons, Arthur Holland-Hibbert, who later became Lord Knutsford, and Lorna Countess Howe. They started the Labrador Club in 1916 and each served as its chairman. Lord Knutsford's Munden Kennels produced the first dogs that showed the Lab's potential in the British field trials, and Lady Howe's dog, Dual Champion Banchory Bolo, became one of the most important dogs of the era. The first Lab entered the United States in 1917, and the first Golden in 1925. But it wouldn't be for many years that either dog would make much of a splash on our shores.

So far we have seen that the Newfoundland "stock" was used in every English retriever that was developed, be it only a "pinch," as in the case of the Golden. When we see what happened to that stock in Newfoundland, it becomes clear that the Malmesbury/Buccleuch line was the only route to survival!

As soon as the Newfoundlanders struck out on their own after the 1713 treaty, they sought ways of making themselves commercially independent. It took more than half a century for them to gain control of the fishing industry, which then became the base of their economy. But the land and the weather made farming almost impossible, and a country needed more than a fishing industry. It was Governor Edwards who in 1780 proposed sheep raising. A law was passed restricting each family to one dog in order to eliminate a menace to the "future" sheep industry. The number of dogs was cut drastically, but then the sheep industry failed to develop. A second such attempt was made in 1885, when a prohibitive tax was placed on dogs, as a supposed danger to sheep. Ten years later Great Britain enacted a six-month quarantine on any dog entering the country. The result was that practically no original stock remained in Newfoundland of either the St. John's Water Dog or the big Newfoundland, and if there were any, they couldn't get into England without a troublesome half-year quarantine.

Even without added stock from Newfoundland, however, there were enough pure lines in Great Britain by this time to supply the demand for this most popular shooting dog. But World War I caused the closing of British kennels. Lord Knutsford's kennel, for one, practically ceased to exist. He started all over again, after the war, with a few puppies.

It was only natural that sooner or later, especially after the near disaster as the result of the Great War, someone would try to find more of the original stock and bring it back to Great Britain in order to infuse fresh blood into the breeding program.

The Search for Fresh Stock from Newfoundland

The seventh duke of Buccleuch and one of his brothers, Lord George Scott, were active in the efforts to bring fresh Labrador blood into the United Kingdom from Newfoundland. In a note from his home in Selkirk, Scotland, the present duke of Buccleuch informs me that the major responsibility for the Buccleuch kennels of Labradors and foxhounds fell on the shoulders of Lord George Scott from the late nineteenth century through the first half of the twentieth. The Buccleuch dogs were not housed in a single kennel but were scattered at various locations in the extensive holdings in southern Scotland and Northamptonshire, which made the family one of the largest landowners in the United Kingdom. The Buccleuch estates at one time employed sixty gamekeepers and owned more than 120 Labradors.

Lord George Scott not only was an expert dog breeder but also was beyond a doubt the first authoritative historian of the Labrador. He produced two very important pieces of writing. The first of these was his chapter on the history of the breed in Leslie Sprake's book *The Labrador Retriever . . . Its History, Pedigrees, Strains, Points, Breeding and Management* (1933). In his chapter, Scott discussed the Newfoundland sheep act of 1885, the disastrous results when the high license rates caused the inevitable destruction of the Labrador females, and the enactment of the six-month quarantine in Britain. Despite these obstacles, he wrote, some British breeders had attempted to import the black Water Dogs from Newfoundland, but had met with little success.

In late 1932, however, Lord George continued, two dogs with the sought-after physical characteristics had been brought to Britain with considerable difficulty. At the time of writing, he said, they were still in quarantine, so it was too early really to assess their qualities.

Scott's second major publication was the book *The Labrador Retriever . . . Its Home and History* (1936), written in collaboration with Sir John Middleton, then the governor of Newfoundland. About 1932 Scott had written to Middleton on behalf of the seventh duke of Buccleuch, enclosing pictures of original Water Dogs, or St. John's dogs, and asking that dogs of this breed be obtained in Newfoundland and shipped over. Middleton turned the assignment over to his aide de camp, Sir Leonard Outerbridge, and after considerable searching a black dog named Cabot and a few others that had the desired looks were located, purchased, and sent to Britain. As usual in Newfoundland, no records of the dogs' ancestry were available. In his 1936 book Scott reported that Cabot's progeny were "first-class water dogs with tender mouths and good noses."

In 1979, however, Lady Jacqueline Barlow of St. John's, Newfoundland, a relative of the queen and a breeder of Newfoundland dogs and

Lord George Scott must be given the major credit for developing the Labrador in the last part of the nineteenth century and bringing the breed into the twentieth century. *(Courtesy of the Duke of Buccleuch)*

member of the Labrador Retriever Club of St. John's, wrote as follows in an article in a newsletter for her club:

> One of the early Water Dog stories in St. John's is told by Sir Leonard Outerbridge. It is the story of Cabot and takes place when he was aide de camp to Governor Sir John Middleton.
>
> Lord George Scott in 1932 wrote to Sir John in Newfoundland and asked him to look out for a dog as per description enclosed, for which he expected to pay 2 pounds. Sir John sent for his Aide, Sir Leonard, and armed with the description in question, Sir Leonard set forth to look for such a dog. Finally after a lengthy and tedious search, Sir Leonard spotted the exact dog of the Duke's description standing on the bow of a fishing boat in St. John's Harbour. Asking if he could buy the dog, offering the 2 pounds, which the skipper readily agreed to as being a princely sum, Sir Leonard stipulated that he must first get the Governor's approval by taking the dog to the government house. This being done, Sir Leonard returned to settle with the skipper of the fishing boat, who, crafty fellow that he was, thought there was obviously more to that particular dog than had met his own eye, upped the price to FIVE pounds! A price the Duke and Lord George Scott incidentally thought excessive, and complained of for many years to Sir John Middleton. In due course the black dog now called "Cabot" (after the discoverer of Newfoundland, John Cabot) was sent to the Duke of Buccleuch.
>
> Sir Leonard quite cheerfully says this splendid specimen of a "Water Dog" had an Alsatian (German Shepherd) for a mother!

The statement that Cabot was a mixed breed, half Water Dog and half German Shepherd, caused sparks to fly across the ocean. The present duke of Buccleuch and Claud Scott, son of Lord George Scott, have rejected this reflection on Cabot's ancestry as unfounded rumor.

Lady Barlow's report of Sir Leonard Outerbridge's story came to my attention while doing the research for my book *The Labrador Retriever . . . The History . . . The People*. To check the story I sent Sir Leonard a copy of what I was going to publish (a reprinting of Lady Barlow's story) and asked him to verify it, and if the story was true to send me a picture of himself to use with it. He was in his early nineties at that time but sent me a handwritten reply, agreeing the story was correct, a mimeographed text about the Lab in Newfoundland, and also his picture, in fact two pictures.

Whatever the facts about Cabot—and I do not wish to take sides at this late date—there can be no doubt whatsoever that Lord George Scott has to

Lady Jacqueline Barlow *(Courtesy of Lady Jacqueline Barlow)*

Sir Leonard Outerbridge *(Courtesy of Sir Leonard Outerbridge)*

be given a major part of the credit for bringing the Labrador into the twentieth century. He started working with the dogs in the family kennels in 1888 and retired in 1946, a year before he died. Starting with only a few, he built the dog to over 150 outstanding specimens. He bred the finest looking and best working dogs in Great Britain in a period when the dog's popularity exploded. Although the credit goes to Lord Knutsford for establishing the Lab in England, because he started the Labrador Retriever Club, the credit for the dogs themselves must go in a big way to Lord George Scott.

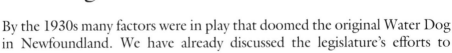

The Second Try at Finding the Lab's "Missing Link"

By the 1930s many factors were in play that doomed the original Water Dog in Newfoundland. We have already discussed the legislature's efforts to establish a sheep industry and the adverse effects of the tax law. There was no Kennel Club in Newfoundland to help keep a line of dogs pure. After World War I, German Shepherds became so popular that they became a street dog and a nuisance. The chance of finding a pure Water Dog or the big Newfoundland on the streets of St. John's or any other well-populated area was very slim. The big Newfoundland dogs had disappeared because they were no longer needed to bring the firewood into town. It was around the 1930s that the last of the few remaining Water Dogs were used by the fishermen.

After reading the original writings of Lord George Scott, I too became interested in finding the original dog in Newfoundland, if possible. On three occasions I had been salmon fishing in the interior of the island, so I had an understanding of the people who lived deep in that isolated, desolate country. There were a number of reasons why it seemed logical that if the dog existed it would have to be in just such an out-of-the-way area.

It was, and still is, a physically tough, hardy people who live in the interior. They have been so isolated for so long that even today they speak a kind of Elizabethan English. We have already explained that their families date back to the early ship jumpers from the fishing fleets. The fisherman's existence was a harsh one, and the British marines were the law. The law of the land was as cruel as the law of the sea. Men and women who jumped ship fled to the interior where they were relatively safe from the marines. (Some joined fighting crews on the pirate ships. Newfoundlanders today whose families can trace their heritage back to the pirates are very proud of their ancestry.) By the end of the eighteenth century, there were hordes of ship jumpers and their offspring living out of the reach of the British Navy. They organized into bands and built roads that ended in swamps so that the marines never could reach them. They had a network of trails that until very recently was used by the postal service as the only means of travel in the interior. For 150 years, they lived in isolation and went so far as to call themselves "the Masterless Men," declaring their independence from the rest of the world. This whole setup was exactly right for finding a dog that had become extinct on the rest of the island. These people were isolated.

Nothing changed their life-style. I found them to be a stubborn, almost illiterate people. There was no reason to believe that they would obey any laws about a tax on their dogs or, for that matter, any other laws. This was the area where even language stood still.

* * *

Understanding the background of the area and the people, my first problem was to get a contact. I wrote to the history and sociology departments of Memorial University of Newfoundland in St. John's explaining my problem and asking for help. Interestingly, I must have written half a dozen letters and all were answered by suggesting that I get in touch with Lady Barlow.

Lady Jacqueline Barlow had come to Newfoundland to live and had brought with her her interest in the Labrador Retriever, which even included some of the queen's yellow Labs. She is very active in the recently formed Labrador Retriever Club. Upon receiving my letter requesting help, she sent me a set of photographs and with it an explanatory letter. She had an exciting story for me. She had just made a holiday trip, by yawl, along the isolated southern coast of Newfoundland. But the photographs were of such poor quality that they needed an explanatory interpretation. She assured me, though, that they were of a true Newfoundland Water Dog. We immediately started a heavy correspondence, and letters were sent off to Harold Melbourne, a contact Lady Barlow had suggested for me in the fishing village of Grand Bruit. Half a year or more went by and I received no answer from Melbourne.

The more I thought about Grand Bruit, the more I realized it fitted the exact pattern of requirements needed to keep dogs isolated from any outside contact. Maps showed no roads to the place.

I had given up hope but wrote again, and a few months later an answer finally came. Melbourne said there were two original dogs left in Grand Bruit. They were brothers, one fifteen and one twelve.

I was soon on a plane north, with a map of Newfoundland in my pocket. The following day, after an overnight ferry trip, I reached Port aux Basques, about fifty miles from Grand Bruit. The only public way to cover these last miles along the desolate southern coast to Grand Bruit was by the government supply boat. I was informed on arrival that it was out of service. As if that weren't enough, a snowstorm hit that kept me motel-bound for three days. The time was put to good use. While all the fishing boats were sitting out the storm, I had the whole fleet trying to find a boat headed along the coast in my desired direction.

I was on board the fifty-two-foot fishing smack *Northern Light* at dawn on the first clear day. Skipper Morgan Durnford and his crew, going up the coast to collect fish for the T. F. Hardy Fish Company, had agreed to deposit me at their second port of call, Grand Bruit.

It was a trip I shall never forget. We hugged the coast all the way, often skirting large boulders. I had an excellent view of the coastline. My binoculars found rock, scrub bush, a few scattered pines—no buildings, or even shacks, no signs of civilization. Hour after hour as we traveled it all seemed better and better. It was this kind of isolation that would be necessary to keep a breeding line pure.

Skipper Durnford was an interesting fellow. I quickly realized he spoke two languages, English to me and another tongue to the crew. At first I thought it might be a dialect of French, but that was not the case. The crewmen living along the isolated coast spoke a sort of Elizabethan English, much like my fishing guides of the interior. I could not understand the seamen nor they me, though it was easy to catch some words we had in common.

The skipper described the Water Dogs his father and grandfather had kept when he was a boy. He kept translating for the hands as we talked. They were much interested in me and our conversation. He praised the dogs for their work in the fishing dories and the sailors agreed. When I asked him why the fishermen no longer used the dog, he stopped and thought for a long time before he answered. He consulted the compass and looked around at some big rocks ahead, then answered with two words, "Better hooks."

What a key answer these two word were! Here was a dog that had earned its keep for centuries by diving overboard to retrieve cod that had thrashed off the hooks as they were brought up to the surface. The dogs lost their place in the world—their job—with the manufacture of better hooks!

Grand Bruit consisted of twenty or so pastel-colored houses scattered in no special order on a rocky formation. An enormous waterfall divided the town, and the church sat on the highest rock. We made our way into the well-protected cove. All the fishermen were waiting on the dock. In fact the whole town turned out. It was easy to spot Harold Melbourne, for a black dog with a white spot on his chest was at his side. This dog—Lassie, a terrible name for such an important, and male, specimen—was truly the "missing link."

The End of the Line

Lassie was a powerful animal even at twelve years of age. His ancestors were the dogs that had been taken to England, starting 180 years ago, to become the Labrador Retriever. Lassie and his line didn't make it. Fortunately he was able to survive as a specimen of his breed because his forebears and he were

Lassie, at Grand Bruit, his isolated home on the southern coast of Newfoundland. Lassie, who is gone now, was the last of the Newfoundland Water Dogs. He was from the original stock. His forebears were sent to England, where they developed and became known as Labradors. *(Author Photo)*

so isolated in this extremely remote part of Newfoundland. In all respects he looked a Lab. He wasn't a show dog; he was built for work.

Unfortunately, because it was a simple fishing village, no one was there to see to the continuation of his line. To the fishermen he was just a dog. Standing with Lassie and watching him retrieve sticks in the ocean with the enthusiasm of a young pup, seeing his desire to please Melbourne, I realized what Lord George Scott had been after. I had found it!

But now it was too late. There were no females and no pups. Lassie was the end of the line. Today he too is gone.

4

The American Scene

As in the fable of the tortoise and the hare, the retrievers in America got a slow and very late start but finally won the race. Today they are the most popular working hunting dogs.

Dogs were always a part of the American scene, but it would be a long time before the outdoor sports scene became part of the average man's life-style. It was a pioneer society built out of what the hands could produce, whether it be on a farm, in a village, in a city, or on the move.

Dogs were on the early scene, but very little has come down to us about them. The explorer de Soto in 1539 had brought some Bloodhounds by way of Cuba to chase the Indians, which certainly was not sport. Howard M. Chapin in 1920 published a book called *Dogs in Early New England* in which he establishes through early records that the first dogs to set foot on New England were two Mastiffs named Foole and Gallant. They were with a landing party in southern Massachusetts in 1603 but actually got no farther than the beach. The dogs were put ashore to sniff around. There was a false alarm of an Indian attack, and they all scurried back to Martin Pring's brig *Discoverer*.

Chapin reports that on the *Mayflower* in 1620 there were two dogs. One was a Mastiff and the other a spaniel. These were the first dogs to become permanent settlers. It seems strange that they didn't bring pairs, but that is what the record shows.

It is not quite clear from Chapin's book whether he thought there was an indigenous dog the Indians had or whether they acquired dogs the white man had brought. The Indian word for dog was *anum.* By the year 1637, both the white man and the Indian were using dogs to prevent surprise attacks. The first recorded incident when dogs were used was at Fort Pequot. According to one Captain Mason, the Indian dogs barked as Mason's men approached, and the Indians cried, *Owanux,* which was their word for Englishmen. The battle commenced. During Queen Anne's War, in Hampshire County, Massachusetts, fifty dogs and fifty soldiers were sent out in small parties to discover and annoy the Indians.

Dogs soon became part of early colonial life. The first dog laws having to do with the protection of farm stock were enacted in Salem in 1635. In 1648, the colony of Massachusetts Bay authorized the purchase of hounds for the destruction of wolves. In 1644 Governor Winthrop told the story of a dog rescuing a Mrs. Dalkin from drowning. The first case of rabies was recorded in 1763. On September 23, 1791, there was an advertisement in the *Providence Gazette* for a lost dog described as a red and white spotted Pointer, with a "tolable long tail," who was owned by John Francis. The dog answered to the name Ponto, and the reward for finding him was four dollars, which was a handsome sum in those days.

Sporting Dogs Come to the American Scene

Thirty years after the Pilgrims landed, the first sporting dogs arrived on the scene. *The American Field,* in its July 23, 1898, issue, reported a celebration held by the Pine Tree Fox Hunting Club of Maryland, commemorating the two hundred and forty-eighth anniversary of the introduction of fox hunting in America. That dates the occasion as 1650.

It was on June 30, 1650, that Mr. Robert Brooke landed in what is now Calvert County, Maryland; he brought with him his wife, ten children, twenty-one manservants, seven maidservants, and his hounds to run fox.

In spite of Brooke, fox hunting was not a popular sport in the early years. It didn't appeal to the Puritans of New England or to the Quakers of Pennsylvania, or to the general population, who thought of fox hunting as the fox being chased by a bunch of hounds, which in turn were chased by a crowd of loafers.

But fox hunting, borrowed directly from England, was to become the sport of the upper class. It took hold with the gentry in colonial America. Even the "Father of His Country" was dedicated to the chase and had his own pack at age twenty. Washington kept a large kennel and meticulous records on his dogs. When he was at Mount Vernon, he rode with the hounds three times a week. He was very sympathetic toward dogs and later taught that attitude to his soldiers.

One story about Washington's respect for dogs should be told. On October 6, 1777, the American army was camped opposite the British near Pennibecker's Mill, Pennsylvania. A lost sporting dog got through the lines and sought food at Washington's headquarters. It was discovered from an engraving on the dog's collar that it belonged to the British commanding officer, General Howe. The American commander-in-chief returned the dog under a flag of truce with a polite note:

> General Washington's compliments to General Howe,—does himself the pleasure to return to him a dog, which accidentally fell into his hands, and, by the inscription on the collar, appears to belong to General Howe.

In return, a letter in the warmest terms was received in the American headquarters.

By the time of the Civil War, fox hunting was the most popular field sport in the country. From Philadelphia to Georgia, from the Eastern Shore of Maryland to the bluegrass region of Kentucky, packs were maintained by the larger landowners, who were the only ones in colonial society who could afford the leisure time. It was a natural result of landowners and their families necessarily being horsemen. A riding horse was their transportation and appropriate to their station in life. A horse suitable for riding around a plantation was equally suitable for following the hounds to the hunt. The rest of America hunted for the pot. Even Abraham Lincoln had a hunting hound.

Early Sporting Literature

The first book on hunting in America was published in New York in 1783. *The Sportsman's Companion* was anonymously written, it is believed, by a former British officer, according to Herm David, dog writer and historian. The book had a very limited circulation. The same can be said about an Italian treatise, *The Method of Raising and Training Pointers,* translated and published in Charleston, South Carolina, in 1799.

Except for the few fox hunters and other men of means, colonial America did not have time for sports. Game birds were rather abundant, and a special dog was not needed to get meat on the table. Hunting was not for sport, it was for the pot.

The first sporting press in America started in 1829. *The American Turf Register and Sporting Magazine* had a major impact by introducing Henry William Herbert, pen name Frank Forester, to American readers. Forester popularized quality dogs with the new but small sporting public. The sportsman, he wrote, needed the company of a quality dog, and he insisted the dog be trained and treated with sympathy and respect.

Before America began to flourish, a dog had to earn its own keep. There were a few English sporting dogs imported by the wealthy, but most dogs were the all-purpose variety: herder and farm "hand," protector, announcer of strangers, family companion, baby-sitter, and hunter. As time was found for the sport of hunting, it was Frank Forester who showed the budding American sportsmen the difference between pot and sport hunting. He introduced them to the ways of the British sporting dogs, their training and care. Forester was a romanticist and sparked many a young man to his new view of the out-of-doors. He was a prolific writer, and his influence was felt for many generations.

By the time Arnold Burges wrote his book *The American Kennel and Sporting Field,* in 1876, a substantial sporting public had developed in Amer-

Henry William Herbert, pen name Frank Forester, popularized outdoor
sports and emphasized the importance of quality dogs.

ica. Incidentally, I do believe that Arnold Burges was actually his name. Most of the important dog writers used pseudonyms. Henry William Herbert took Forester as his pen name because he thought writing about the shooting sports and dogs was beneath the dignity of a serious writer, who should not be identified with such matters. Most of the early American writers hid their identity behind a fictitious signature to avoid the censure of ultramoralists in the land of our Puritan forefathers. But strangely, the same use of pseudonyms occurred in England, where there were no "blue laws."

Burges in his book uses the writings of Stonehenge (John H. Walsh), Idstone (Reverend Mr. Pearce), and Dinks (Captain Peel) to make a strong bid to the American sportsman to use the English Setter for his hunting. He gives some interesting facts about the setter. The setter is a direct descendant of the Land Spaniel, and the Setting Spaniel (which no longer exists) is really the first setter. It's an old breed. Stonehenge claims that "A Duke of Northumberland trained one to set birds in 1555, and shortly after the setter was produced." Idstone claims the setter followed the Romans or was brought to England by them.

Richard Surflet in 1600 wrote of the setter, ". . . they must hunt close and mute. And when they come on the haunt of that they hunt, they shall sodainely stop and fall down on their bellies, and so creep by degrees to the game till they come within two or three yards thereof, or so neare that they cannot press nearer without danger of retrieving. Then shall youre setter stick, and by no persuasion go further till yourself come in and use your pleasure."

The English Setter Takes Its Place

Burges describes one by one most of the hunting dogs available to the English and American hunter, but then has this to say:

> If a man lives in a country abounding in small patches of thick cover and is not a good enough shot to kill his birds therein, let him use a spaniel to drive the birds out; if he lives in a hot, dry country and never shoots elsewhere, a

pointer will suit him best; but if he wants a dog for all kinds of work, and over which he can kill every variety of game bird with the least regard to cover, footing, or temperature, let him get a high-couraged, pure-blooded English Setter, intelligently handle and break him, treat him well, and fear no form of dog that can be brought against him. Such a dog I pronounce the best animal for American upland shooting.

Burges points out that the setter has another attribute. For the occasional duck hunter, the setter makes a fine retriever. J. W. Long, a noted waterfowler in the Midwest in Burges's day, speaks very highly of the setter as a retriever. The point is being made that the setter is the American dog, the dog everyone used, unless, as Burges points out, you live and hunt in the Chesapeake area.

Burges tells us that "Since the war the Chesapeake from neglect have become very scarce." This is an interesting fact, because none of the modern Chessie writers even mentions that, according to Burges, "A number of prominent duck shooters established a kennel to bring them up to their former standard." He advises that the Chesapeake Bay Retriever is "unsurpassed if equaled at all in the world." He adds that "The use of retrievers as a specialty is almost exclusively confined to the neighborhood of Chesapeake Bay, since in the West most of the fowl shooting is done in localities that setters have hitherto answered all purposes where dogs are needed."

It is interesting to note that Burges never mentions the American Water Spaniel, known in his day as simply the Water Spaniel.

So the stage has been set for the American hunter by both Frank Forester and then Arnold Burges that the sportsman, except in special circumstances, needed as his first choice an English Setter. At that time, with the abundance of game, this was very good advice.

For the next half century, the literature became abundant and so did the pointing breeds. The classics of the shotgun sports became quail shooting over Pointers in the South and grouse and woodcock over setters in the North. At this time in Victorian England, the retrievers were being developed for the pass shooting of driven birds.

We have pointed out that on the English scene Colonel Peter Hawker's book of 1814, *Instructions to a Young Sportsman,* had an important impact on many generations of young hunters. In America, when the society was ready, both economically and socially, a new class-conscious society had similar books for their young men. One good example was Maurice Thompson's *The Boys' Book of Sports and Outdoor Life,* published in New York in 1886. In charming, nineteenth-century story-telling form, instructions and information on just about every phase of outdoor sports were given. Every red-blooded young man wanted an English Setter named Don, like the one the heroes of Thompson's story, Neil and Hugh, had as they brought down quail and grouse. Starting those desires while young and having them fed with the new outdoors magazines that appeared on the scene, like *Forest and Field* (later called *Field and Stream*) and *Sports Afield* and many more, made America a field-conscious nation.

Interestingly, retrievers are not even mentioned in the Thompson book.

The Brown Winchester or Red Chester— an American Breed?

At the time of the Burges book, in 1876, a Mr. O. D. Foulks, a well-known and accomplished sportsman of Chesapeake City, Maryland, and a correspondent of the *American Sportsman,* wrote about an American retriever called the Brown Winchester or Red Chester.

It is difficult from Foulks's writing, as quoted by Burges, to tell whether the Brown Winchester or Red Chester is a breed that was developed in the Chesapeake area and lost, or whether Foulks was writing about the Chesapeake Bay Retriever itself. The presentation is ambiguous. But it is hard to believe that a knowledgeable sportsman would have confused the two. The Chessie was well known by this time. As early as 1845, an American sporting book called *The Dog and the Sportsman,* published in Philadelphia, had a fine chapter on the Chesapeake Bay Water Dog. In that book, written by J. S. Skinner, the story of the Chessie's origins is reported in the famous letter signed by George Law describing the sinking of the English brig, "which was bound to Poole in England from Newfoundland. I found on board of her two Newfoundland pups, male and female, which I saved. . . . I purchased these pups from the captain for a guinea apiece. I gave the dog pup, which was called 'Sailor,' to Mr. John Mercer of West River, and the slut pup, which was called 'Canton,' to Dr. James Stewart." And so the story of the

Chesapeake Bay Retriever started. The dog became so popular and the story so well known that we have to assume that O. D. Foulks's writings were about another American retriever that did not survive.

Foulks writes: "The only real ducking dog, bred and raised for the purpose, which can stand the cold and fatigue for any length of time, is the Brown Winchester or Red Chester, a cross between the English Water Poodle and the Newfoundland." The Water Poodle we can assume is the same as the English Rough Water Dog. This dog has never been associated with the background of the Chesapeake Bay Retriever. He continues:

> They are a low, heavy set, densely coated dog, of dark reddish brown color on the back, shading lighter on the sides, and running into a very light yellow or white on the belly and inside the legs: the throat and breast are frequently marked with white. They are of other colors, but any change from the brown shows a want of careful breeding. This breed I am sorry to say, is fast going out of existence. At one time they were very common here, almost every person living on a ducking shore owning one or two, but the war coming on scattered the old families, and the newcomers, either not knowing the value of the breed, or else not taking an interest in anything outside the farm, have allowed it to run almost entirely out.

Note that this is the same thing that happened to the Chesapeake Bay Retriever at this time. The colors of the Chessie were not completely set by this time. That is why the question of what dog the author is discussing arises.

Foulks continues:

> This breed of dogs are very swift and powerful swimmers, they will chase a crippled duck one or two miles, and unless the duck is very slightly hit, will catch him in the end. The dog sits on the shore behind a blind, his color matching so well with the sand and clay that were he even continually moving the ducks would never notice him (this is the reason the color is so carefully bred for). He seldom moves any part of his body except his head, which he continually turns up and down the river, often sighting the approaching ducks before the gunner. When the gun is fired and a duck falls, he bounds to the edge of the water, plunges in and brings it ashore, and then without having received a word of command from his master, carries it up to the place where he sits and drops it. After giving himself two or three shakes and a roll, he resumes his old station and watch. He does not shiver like a setter, or raise

and drop his fore-feet like a wet spaniel; the shaking he has given his coarse, oily coat, has freed it entirely from ice and water; he can not be enticed into a kennel, but must sit out on the frozen shore, rain or shine, as well as the gunner. If one of the fallen birds chance to be only crippled, he swims past the dead ones, keeping the wounded duck in sight; when it dives he swims to the spot and there continues turning round and round, now and then throwing himself high in the water, especially if the waves are heavy. As soon as the duck reappears, he strikes out immediately for it, and as it dives again he swims to the spot where he last saw it, and continues to turn until the duck comes up, then another swim, and so on until the duck is tired out or escapes him. If the duck falls too far out for the dog to see, he takes his direction from the motion of the hand. . . .

This appears to be the first real description of a working retriever at work. This is also the first mention of handling in the literature: "He takes his direction from the motion of the hand." One of the frustrating things about dog research is that most writers never seem to stop and do what O. D. Foulks has done, that is, describe the dog plus his work in the field. Foulks continues:

The spaniel and the setter are often used when the Winchester cannot be had. They make a good substitute while they last, which is not very long. They cannot stand the ice-cold water and frozen shores, day in day out the season through; spaniels are too small to stand the heavy waves, and setters are not heavy coated, rheumatism attacks them in a year or two, followed by a gathering in the head which destroys their hearing and finally ends their lives. Other water dogs may be used, but the difficulty is in breaking them to understand the difference between a duck and a block of wood. I have seen many dogs called ducking dogs, which at the report of a gun would bound into the water and bring out a decoy, if a duck had not fallen, or they could not find it immediately.

There are two things about that last paragraph that we wish the author had elaborated upon. He writes, "Other water dogs may be used." It would be interesting to know which ones he was referring to. Was he talking about the Chessie when he said they were difficult in breaking? The Chessie is noted for being hardheaded. The other thing I wish he had explained was, "The spaniel and the setter are often used. . . ." What spaniel was he talking about? Was it a water spaniel? Could it have been the American Water Spaniel?

The American Water Spaniel— Another American Dog

The American Water Spaniel is American-made, but no one knows exactly how it was done.

When the dog was recognized by the American Kennel Club in 1940, the *American Kennel Gazette* carried an article to inform its members of the latest dog to be recognized. Not a word was mentioned about the dog's

The American Water Spaniel, the Indian dog that got its start in the Midwest just after the Civil War *(Author Photo)*

background. Thirty-six years later the *Gazette* tried to guess at the dog's past. They put it this way:

> The American Water Spaniel appears to have been developed in the Fox and Wolf River area near Oshkosh, Wisconsin, and for many years was found only in that region.
>
> It is difficult to trace the precise origins, but the principal ingredients in achieving the mix were the English Water Spaniel (a breed now extinct), the Irish Water Spaniel, and the Curly-Coated Retriever. It is possible that the Sussex Spaniel also may have played a part in the development of the American Water.

The mention of the Sussex Spaniel was most likely a wild guess by the *AKC Gazette.* They give no proof or explanation, and the possibility of the Sussex being involved is never mentioned again in the literature.

Sixteen-month-old American Water Spaniel Champion Just Plain Ol' Lucy, owned by John and Susan Liemohn, at Lake Kabetogama in northern Minnesota *(Photo by John Liemohn)*

The story of the dog's origin depends on what book you read. The *Spaniel Owner's Encyclopedia* by John F. Gordon says that the dog was "undoubtedly created from the Irish Water Spaniels." C. Bede Maxwell's fine book, *The Truth About Sporting Dogs,* states that the American Water Spaniel "is poles apart from the Irish Water Spaniel." Pay your money and take your pick. If I were a betting man, I might even suggest that a chocolate Poodle (called a brown by the Poodle folks) might have gotten into the act. No one seems to suggest that, yet it is as good a guess as any of the other writers have had, including the *AKC Gazette.* Dave Duffy, the well-known dog writer, who comes from the area where the dog originated and was a personal friend of "Doc" Pfiefer, the "father" of the American Water Spaniel, seems to know more about the breed than anyone else. He firmly believes that the Irish Water Spaniel was not in the background of the American. He writes that according to Pfiefer the Irish was introduced into the dog after Pfiefer had registered the first American Water Spaniel and was breeding them successfully.

There has run through the literature the romantic notion that Columbus brought a pair of spaniels with him that became the American Water Spaniel. It seems very unlikely. With his problems of falling off the edge of the world and all that sort of thing, it does seem strange that Columbus would be bothered with a brace of spaniels. Besides, all agree that the dog was developed in the middle of the United States, and the Midwest is a big "sail" from the Caribbean.

The Columbus story is not very believable. The dog writers can't have their cake and eat it too. On one hand, they claim the dog is made up of a mix of nineteenth-century English dogs; on the other hand, the dogs came to America on a fifteenth-century ship.

A more reasonable story seems to be that some sort of a water spaniel got into the Midwest and was used by the Indians and a number of the half-breed settlers. After the Civil War, when the movement was westward, the dog was discovered by the new settlers, who needed a dog for all purposes. Since this was a very heavy waterfowl area, hunting for the table and the newfangled notion of hunting for sport required a good dog. A small one made sense. The Indian dog was used, and the early settlers mixed it with whatever—and that is the big argument—to give it a tighter coat to protect it against the cold water.

Just as in the case of the Chesapeake Bay Retriever, where the farmer-sportsman developed the dog and then it was taken over by the watermen, in the case of the American Water Spaniel the original Indian dog was developed by the settlers into the American Water Spaniel and then the Indians used it extensively. It became known as the "Indian dog." In the early part of the twentieth century, it reverted to become the "white man's dog" just as the Chessie became the sportsman's dog.

For some reason, then, at the turn of the century, when hunting for sport increased, the dog's popularity waned. The reason might have been that the concept of one dog for each type of hunting was becoming popular. The little forty-pound, closely curled, liver or dark chocolate fellow was most versatile; he'd hunt and retrieve all game, both fur and feather; but he wasn't a specialist.

"Doc" Pfiefer Befriends the American Water Spaniel

The first person associated with the dog to have his name passed down to us was "Doc" Pfiefer of New London, Wisconsin. Doc, officially F. T. Pfiefer, M.D., grew up in the Wolf River area and started practicing medicine in New London in 1909. His father, interested in dogs, kept Mastiffs, and as an infant Doc fooled around with their food pans; it is said that he carried scars on his legs all his life. This did not seem to lessen his interest in dogs. At fourteen he trained a St. Bernard to pull him around in a dog cart. His father put the boy, the dog, and the cart on a train to visit some relatives in Milwaukee. Doc recalled the story as a real happening. This was before the advent of the motorcar, and when he hitched up the dog and drove from the station to his relatives' home, traffic came to a standstill.

Doc wrote:

> I have read so many conflicting articles about the origin of the American Water Spaniels in different complete dog books and encylopedias that I would like to give the true facts about their recognition as a separate breed.

My father, who owned a small city drug store in Plymouth, Wisconsin, in 1876, was visited by many Indians of various tribes. They came to buy and barter for supplies and tobacco. Most of them were accompanied by dogs but predominantly the so-called American Water Spaniel. My father called them Indian Dogs.

In 1891 I came home with a small American Water Spaniel given to me by a friend. My father said, 'What do you want with that Indian Dog?' In 1892 I borrowed a single 12 gauge shot gun and my friend and I went hunting every Saturday and Sunday. My dog would run rabbits and tree many partridges. We came home with enough game for our neighbors. I always had American Water Spaniels when I was a boy.

In 1919 I wrote the A.K.C. and told them I knew these dogs always bred true to form and conformation and the litters were like peas in a pod and that I wanted to register them. Naturally, with no background, they turned me down. I then wrote to the Field Stud Book with the same results. In 1920 I wrote to the United Kennel Club of Kalamazoo, Michigan, giving the lineage and background of this fine hunting dog. They registered Curly Pfiefer on April 8, 1920, as the first American Spaniel registered.

After five generations of registration in the United Kennel Club or a purple ribbon, as they call it, the Field and Stud Book registered them. In 1940 the A.K.C. accepted them as a separate breed.

Doc lived into his nineties and for many decades was a most important figure on the dog scene in the Midwest.

There were several attempts, starting as far back as 1881, to form an American Water Spaniel club, but the first successful one didn't appear until 1937. The first president was Driscoll O. Scanlan of Nashville, Illinois. He was the foremost breeder of the day and did some writing about the dog. Shortly after the formation of the club, the *Field Dog Stud Book,* in 1938, accepted the dog for registration.

Reading through every possible document I could get my hands on, both printed material and private letters, I learned that the story of the dogs' coming over with Columbus seems to have been something that Scanlan "invented." True or not, the story was a brilliant piece of public relations for the dog. The story has been quoted hundreds of times in print.

During World War II, the club became defunct, and the disruption caused a major setback for the American Water Spaniel.

At first glance you might think the dog affectionately called "Brownie,"

"Curly," "Water Spaniel," or "American Brown" was more of a retriever than a spaniel. Actually it is in-between. It is just as much at home in a duck blind as it is quartering a field for upland game. On land it works in the classical spaniel manner, flushing game to the gun, marking the fall, then retrieving. It is said that on quail the dog can in many cases be taught to hold before flushing. It is a kind of point, giving the hunter time to move up and flush the game himself. On water it can be taught the game as the Labrador plays it. It is classed by the AKC as a spaniel, possibly because of its size. This classification all these years has prevented the American Water Spaniel from entering the AKC retriever events. Tom Olsen, the president of the newly formed American Water Spaniel breed club, considers this a major problem and says the members of the club are divided: some want the dog classified as a retriever. Actually, this is another example of organizations like the AKC and their politics getting in the way. The dog should be able to run in any kind of a field event if it has the ability. The American Water Spaniel is included in this book on retrievers because it is a good working fellow in a duck blind or marsh, no matter what its classification.

Here is what Duffy wrote before the formation of the North American Hunting Retriever Association about the American Water Spaniel:

> He should be more popular, but he isn't for two reasons. One, he is not a pretty dog and because most of his breeders and users have been practical hunting men, the American has never caught on for the show ring. Secondly, despite his strong natural inclination to hunt and retrieve which makes training easy, there is no niche in the field trial world, with its attendant publicity for the American. Capable of a dual role as a waterfowl retriever and upland game flusher to an extent that he would satisfy most hunters, he isn't large enough to compete with the Labradors, Chesapeakes and Goldens in the retriever trials, or dashing enough to shine when pitted against a springer in a spaniel trial.

Tell that to an old-timer and he'd give "Brownie" higher points. Here is a dog he hunted hard and bragged about, who followed the kids to school and did parlor tricks for Aunt Mabel or saloon patrons. Another of its successes: it is the official dog of the state of Wisconsin.

Another Spaniel, the Boykin

Ever since George Washington threw a "cartwheel" across the Rappahannock River, the silver dollar has even become part of the legends of our home-bred American retrievers.

Back in the days of the market hunter, a silver dollar would buy four or five frying chickens and as much beef as you would want to carry home, according to a story Ray Holland, one of our great outdoor writers, told about the American Water Spaniel. In those days, there was an old Missouri River market hunter by the name of Frank Dougherty who was a fantastic

The Boykin Spaniel stands only about fifteen inches high and weighs about thirty pounds, but has the drive of a dog three times its size. *(Author Photo)*

duck shot and had an American Brown as his working partner. The dog weighed only thirty-five pounds, but duck or geese, it made no difference. He'd grab a Canada goose by the wing tip or the neck and drag the heavy bird out on shore.

The dog had an uncanny nose, and Frank used to do a stunt to show off his partner to his friends. He'd take a silver dollar and rub it well in the palm of his hand; then showing it to the dog he'd throw the "cartwheel" as far as he could into the cornfield. We do not know if the throw was as far as Washington's, but the dollar meant more to Frank than to George since he wasn't very wealthy; he got only ten cents a bird at the market. Money was something to take care of, yet Frank would throw it into the corn grown up in weeds with as much concern as if he were throwing a rock. Of course you know the rest of the story—the dog dashed into the field and never failed his partner.

On the Eastern Shore of Maryland, where the Chessie originated, a silver dollar today will just about pay for only one oyster on the half shell, but back in the market hunter's day, an "iron man" was a good day's pay. The story goes that the watermen played a betting game. A silver dollar was thrown overboard, and one at a time the dogs dove for it. The man who threw in the silver had first chance with his dog and if successful kept running his dog on the next fellow's dollar till the dog failed. I always figured it was legend and about as possible as the original George Washington story at the Rappahannock . . . until I saw it done in six to eight feet of water.

The last American-bred retriever is the Boykin Spaniel, and it too gets involved with the "cartwheel," if only in a "tall tale." Cathy J. Flamholtz tells the yarn in her book, *A Celebration of Rare Breeds* (1986):

A very long time ago, there was a man with a small spaniel that was an excellent retriever. The man trained his little dog to fetch a silver dollar and that dog would pursue the coin wherever it was thrown. No matter how dense the brush, how high the cornfield or thick the pasture grass, that little fellow would find and retrieve the coin. Well, one day the man was showing off for a stranger and he flung that coin as far as he could into the woods. A young boy happened to be walking through the woods and he picked up the shiny silver dollar and tucked it into his pocket. But that didn't deter the little dog. In his zeal to obey his master, he brought the coin home, boy and all. And that, my friends, is how the dog got his name. . . . the dog didn't retrieve it but the boy-can . . . thus, Boykin.

That story still gets told in South Carolina with tongue in cheek.

The Boykin Spaniel exploded on the hunting scene only a dozen years ago. He won the hearts of the South Carolinians, has become their state dog, and is now making his bid all over the country. As retrievers go, he's a half-pint. He's less than half the size of a Labrador Retriever, weighing in around thirty-five pounds, and stands only about fifteen inches high, take a couple more or less. Energy? Uncontainable. He's explosive in the field, and a hunter's delight, but as docile as a lamb with kids around the house. He's a cute little fellow with big, floppy ears, making him a favorite with mothers.

Where did the little fellow come from? With a bit of investigation, we're going to unravel that. Like no other hunting retriever, he was made by committee from a very mixed-up background. That happened in 1977. Although he had had his name for half a century, no one seemed to know how to "make him," or for that matter, what he was made of or what he should look like. But a lucky fluke in his story changed all that. Today the Carolinian dog is making his mark.

The little dog's beginnings are almost as American as southern grits and cornbread. Picture a lazy Sunday morning on East Main Street in Spartanburg, South Carolina. Alec White, born in 1860, was somewhere in his mid-forties on that particular Sunday. He was walking to the First Presbyterian Church, two blocks away, to meet his family, who had gone on ahead. Out of the corner of his eye he noted that he was being followed by a tiny brownish, or maybe reddish, curly-haired pup. He could hear the congregation singing, but not exactly being in a terrible hurry, he stopped and had a one-sided conversation with the little fellow. Then a few friendly pats were issued to send the pup on his way home.

After church—and it is believed Alec left early—there was the floppy-eared, newly acquired friend waiting. Man and dog walked together back to 481 East Main Street for Sunday dinner.

There is nothing unusual about a stray dog's being taken home and becoming a member of the family, but this chance occurrence had important consequences. The Boykin would never have made its debut except for a warm, strong friendship that began in the late 1800s between two South Carolina gentlemen and sportsmen: that same Alexander Lawrence White,

It was at the First Presbyterian Church in Spartanburg, South Carolina, that the Boykin got its start, when Alec White took note of the little brown stray dog. *(Courtesy of Pete Rose)*

president of the Farmers and Merchants Bank of Spartanburg, and Lemuel Whittaker Boykin, planter, land appraiser, and sportsman of Plain Hill, about ten miles from Camden, South Carolina.

Although they lived one hundred miles apart, as teenagers both Alec and Whit had courted Lavolette McGowan. Both men were keen hunters and conservationists way ahead of their time. They started a group called the South Carolina Sportsmen's Society with another of their hunting buddies, John Manning Cantey, who married into the Boykin family. They subscribed to mandatory bag limits on Tom turkeys, no shooting of hens, and a daily limit on quail, quite an advance for that day.

Alec White and Whit Boykin hunted together constantly, and as they matured, Whit's daughter recalls, "My father loved Alec White, who we called Uncle Knox, like a brother." They wrote to each other once a week, and if a letter did not arrive, something was wrong. The Boykin Spaniel was "born" out of this fast friendship.

Historically, it can be demonstrated that for a dog to become a popular,

successful hunting breed, it not only has to have a purpose and be good at
that work, but just as important, the dog must be sponsored by men of
position, means, and social standing in the community. A good example of
this is the Labrador in nineteenth-century England, where its benefactors
were dukes and earls. In the twentieth century, the Lab's earliest sponsors
in this country were America's wealthiest families. The Boykin has been
developed and coddled by southern gentry.

The Boykins are an old South Carolina family going back to Jarvis
Boykin, a carpenter from Charing Cross, London, England, who arrived in
Charleston with one servant in 1635. Another Boykin, Edward, received a
land grant in 1685, but the bulk of the vast family land holdings was
acquired later by Burwell Boykin as recompense received for services during
the Revolution. Captain Alexander Hamilton Boykin was a decorated hero
during the War Between the States. The Boykins were a wealthy, socially
prominent, distinguished family.

During the early part of this century, the area of Camden and nearby
Boykin Community became popular as a winter resort for the social set.
Wealthy Yankees came there to play. Those who loved outdoor sports
sought an invitation from the Boykins, three generations of them, to float
the Wateree River for some very sporty duck hunting. Great friendships were
started and survived many hunting seasons. The little dog Whit and his
hunting cronies developed into a hunting retriever made a big hit, and many
a pup went back to Yankee land at the end of the season.

The dog that was to come into being and be known as the Boykin
Spaniel had its purpose cut out for it before the dog was even found. Out
of necessity, both Alec White and Whit Boykin had been looking for some
twenty years, starting in the 1880s, for a small dog that could do the specific
work required for their type of hunting.

Hunting South Carolina's Wateree River before the turn of the century
required a rugged dog with many talents. These men were turkey and duck
hunters, and the river was the only means of transport through the swampy
areas. The dog had to be a good water retriever and a close hunting dog.
Besides water work, retrieving ducks, the dog had to have a fine nose and
be fast enough to trail and flush wild turkeys, but not to scatter them too
far as a big dog will do.

The only thoroughfare through this area of thickets, rich with game,
was the water. This was before the day of outboard motors and trailers, so
a small boat was needed. The local hunters designed a three-section boat that

was fastened together with bolts. It could be taken apart and loaded on a wagon for transport to and from the river. On short float trips a wagon would meet the hunting party downriver. Overnight floats would be made to the nearest railroad head, where the boat could be unbolted, taken apart, and loaded onto a train, with all the rest of the gear and dogs, for the return trip home to Boykin.

But the dog they had to use, through the turn of the century, the Chesapeake Bay Retriever, caused many a problem. Bringing an eighty- to one-hundred-pound dog, with a mallard in its mouth, back into the boat could mean a ducking for all.

It was almost useless to hunt this area without a dog to retrieve the game. As the boat was paddled or floated downstream, the waterfowl would flush out of the reeds and foliage, often to be downed farther back in the swamp. A good dog was a must. What Whit Boykin, John Cantey, and Alec White talked about was a little dog. A dog that wouldn't take up so much space in the wagon, or on the train, and, most important, in the boat. A dog that, if it did shift position, was not a threat to all the hunters and their gear. They wanted a small dog that could dive overboard and not rock the boat, a sure retriever that when it swam back to the floating boat could be lifted with one hand, by the scruff of the neck, out of the water and into the boat in one fell swoop, duck and all.

Almost a hundred miles from the Wateree River, over in Spartanburg, the little dog that came to Sunday dinner was named Dumpy because of his small size in comparison with the retrievers and bird dogs that were already a part of Alec White's kennel. Size didn't seem to bother Dumpy, for he managed to hold his own with the big dogs. Mr. White noted that the little fellow had a remarkable aptitude for retrieving anything, whether it was thrown or just because the dog found and carried about in his mouth.

One day, as a lark, Mr. White took Dumpy duck hunting along with his Chesapeakes. Little Dumpy was so fast and agile that he beat the retrievers at their own game. That's when things started to click. Dumpy was shipped off to friend Whit Boykin, who was an excellent trainer. It was suggested that Dumpy had the natural instinct and ability, was the right size, and just might answer their need for a small duck and turkey dog on the Wateree.

This was after the turn of the century, possibly as late as 1909 or 1910. According to Whit's daughter, Wrennie, Dumpy immediately became Pappa's favorite, and was the only dog of all the kennel that was given Boykin house privileges. The dog proved to be ideal for the Wateree River; he was an ardent duck and turkey dog.

The Boykin Spaniel
Starts with Dumpy

Whit Boykin was so pleased with Dumpy's work that word was spread through the family and among their friends to try to find a small reddish or brown mate for Dumpy. It was advertised in the church bulletin. The search was called off when a promising-looking female was found by a railroad porter. A curly-haired, dark reddish-brown dog of uncertain breeding was left unclaimed at the station in a baggage crate. She was sent to Whit Boykin, who named her Singo. The Boykin Spaniel supposedly started from this mating.

Although today the Boykin is used for duck and dove hunting, in the early part of the century, it was used primarily as a turkey dog. Back then, the duck hunting on the Wateree River and swamps was a by-product of the turkey hunting. The only way to the turkey-hunting grounds was downriver. To get there the hunters floated through some of the best mallard jump-shooting in the East. When they reached the area where turkey flocks were known to feed, a line of hunters would spread out through the woods and find concealment behind brush. Then a few hunters with Boykins went downstream and entered the woods, working back toward the hunters. The dogs quartering ahead scoured the ground, and when turkey scent was found the little dogs went into high gear. Boykins are high-strung hunters and operate on upland game like no other dogs. They run around almost like maniacs, working frantically. They got the job done, and the big birds took to the air as their only escape route. The hunters shot only Toms, and the dogs, giving tongue, pursued the downed, wounded birds trying to escape.

The other way the Boykin was used on turkey was in "still hunting," and that cost the dog its tail. The hunter and his Boykin would walk through a likely patch of cover. When the dog found the scent, it charged in and the birds flushed in every direction. Once the birds were scattered, the hunter built himself a small blind to conceal himself and the dog. Man and dog had to stay completely hidden, motionless, and absolutely silent except for the turkey-calling device, which enticed the birds back to the feeding area. Hunters could teach the dog to sit quietly and watch the birds coming back into gun range, but they could not stop that excited tail from wagging. There wasn't enough room in a blind for man, dog, and a swishing tail that rustled every twig and leaf within reach. Off came the tail.

There are no surviving records of how the Boykin family bred the early Boykins or even a good description of what they looked like. The Boykin family believe for sure that Alec and Whit put some Chesapeake Bay Retriever into the mix and possibly a dash of Springer and maybe Pointer. But this is all their educated guess. You cannot tell much from the pictures that have survived for half a century or more.

I have been able to find only two references to the dog in print until it became popular in 1975. The first story appeared in 1943 when one of the visiting sportsmen, Jack Forster, whom Whit recalls as being a New York publishing executive, wrote a two-column story about the Boykin Spaniel for Arnold Gingrich, the sportsman editor of *Esquire* magazine.

The second came in 1969 when a staff writer on the Spartanburg *Journal,* Bud Siefert, did a fifteen-part series on pets, of whom the Boykin was one. And that was all the outside world knew about the Boykin Spaniel.

The Boykin Spaniel Society

There are two distinct Boykin eras. The first era started with the puppy outside the church in Spartanburg and ended shortly after World War II when the South Carolina wintering resort lost some of its appeal for affluent visiting Yankees.

Between the two years was a period from the end of the war to the early 1970s, when the dog almost disappeared. This often happens in the dog world. Dogs are like designer clothes: tastes and fads change. The dogs that were taken north by the visiting sportsmen more or less disappeared. Only the Boykin family kept the breed going for their own hunting. Then a series of events changed the dog's future.

The second era started in 1975 with the writings of Mike Creel, a very competent researcher and outdoor writer. The results of his work brought about the need for the Boykin Spaniel Society.

Creel, who had a real knack for history and research, figured the Boykin would make a fascinating story. This was in the early 1970s, and Creel says that at the time, except for the few dogs the Boykin family had, he could hardly find any to write about. The more he researched the story the more fascinated he became by the local color of the fashionable hunting era that had just passed. He decided that one way to tell the story of this whole era that seemed to be slipping away was through this little dog who was truly a South Carolina product.

Creel talked to anyone he could find, old or young, who remembered the dog. He especially interviewed the Boykins and their kin. He took his idea to the *South Carolina Wildlife* magazine. He says they turned it down, saying that there were so few of the dogs around that they didn't think the public would be interested.

A fluke series of events changed all of that. Not long after Creel suggested the story to the magazine, a professional trainer in Boykin, Bruce Jackson, who knew the Boykin family, raised one of their pups more or less as a lark. Jackson had a wide reputation as a trainer of hunting Labradors. When his Boykin had pups, he placed them with friends. One pup went to John Culler, the editor of *South Carolina Wildlife*. John trained the pup, named Lucky, and claims even today that Lucky was the best dove-hunting dog he ever had. Outdoor writer Mike Creel dusted off his Boykin story and offered it again. This time it "flew," farther than anyone's expectations.

The story tickled the fancy of the South Carolinians. This was their dog! The fervor was such that eventually the South Carolina legislature voted the Boykin Spaniel their state dog.

Immediately on publication of Creel's story in the September/October 1975 issue of the *South Carolina Wildlife,* there was an explosive demand for the "new" fellow, who had to be trained by love and had a heart for his work as big as his thirty-five pounds.

But the problem that had plagued the pup from that first Sunday in Spartanburg, some seventy years earlier, came close to destroying it: no one knew its exact heritage. By this time, some pups, even in the same litter, were curly-coated, some were wavy-coated, some were short- and smooth-haired.

Some pups were leggy, some were short, some were black, some had white markings, while most were dark chocolate or rich brown. The magazine article created a demand from a public that didn't even know what the dog should look like. And at that time, with very few breeders, few litters being produced, demand outstripped supply. But for money—anything was sold as a Boykin Spaniel pup.

A typical example of what was happening is told by Camden, South Carolina, veterinarian Peter McKoy, who, although he never owned a Boykin, is responsible for getting the Boykin Spaniel Society started:

When I started my practice I didn't see too many Boykins. But I had one client who was very much interested in the dog's temperament and conformation. That was Baynard Boykin, and when he produced a litter, if he saw something that he figured his Granddaddy wouldn't be very proud of, that animal did not continue on as a breeding animal. That is where it stopped, right there.

After that *Wildlife* magazine article, pups were selling for as much as two hundred dollars. Well, any time the price of meat goes up by fifty percent you get poachers. That started people thinking so anything started to pass as Boykins. One woman came into my office with her brown Poodle who by accident had been bred to a Boykin, she thought. I took care of the pups. There were two browns and two blacks. Six weeks later when she brought the pups in for shots, she only had the two blacks. I asked her where the two browns were and she said she'd sold them for Boykin Spaniels for $200.00 each. That didn't sit right in my craw, but the *coup de grace* happened later that day when Baynard Boykin brought in a pup to be put to sleep. His family had been breeding the dog for generations and that pup had something about it that he didn't think was good for the line. It was put down.

I was slapped right up against it! That started gnawing on me. If the folks who were being very selective in their breeding knew what I knew they would have a hard time of it and Baynard's Granddaddy, ol' Whit Boykin, would turn over in his grave if he knew some lady was selling brown, half Poodles as Boykins. I felt obligated, because it was not right that because of demand and the money . . . some folks were destroying the work the Boykins were doing, keeping a line of hunting dogs going. So I contacted Baynard and his cousin Whit. That's where the idea started to form a club before things got out of hand.

Whit and Baynard told me that they had tried to start a club prior to this but couldn't get it going because everyone had their own idea of what the dog should look like and most of the club members would have been Boykin family

The Boykin is a fine working retriever on both upland birds and waterfowl. (*Author photo*)

and like most families, they couldn't agree on anything, let alone the hair on a dog.

A few years after Mike Creel's story appeared in South Carolina, the magazine's editor, John Culler, went to New York to become the editor of *Outdoor Life,* one of the "big three" hunting and fishing magazines. Culler recalls that he and his dog Lucky hated New York, and after only two years they went back south to edit *Sporting Classics* magazine. But while in New York he had Mike Creel dust off the old Boykin story again, and through *Outdoor Life* the dog received national attention. The Boykin and its story were so attractive that in a short time there were Boykins in every state in the Union.

Culler, who is responsible for giving all the editorial attention to the Boykin, made a strange statement in my presence. Later it took much research and pondering to understand what he said: "I don't believe there is any such thing as a Boykin Spaniel!"

But with all the publicity the trouble really begins. We have a dog that is considered a separate breed, but there is no written standard. The dog gets public acceptance, and nobody knows what it should be or what its pups should look like. Everyone had his or her own ideas. It was perhaps stated best recently by a local workman standing, first on one foot then on the other, in front of an electric heater at the Wooten "store" on route 421 outside of Boykin, "It should be a small brown dog that's a hell of a hunter."

Since the dog was a mix and no one knew just what the mix was, the society set out to try to save their dog. For the first time ever, a dog will be developed by committee. What a problem they had! Those who owned wavy-coated dogs wanted that as the standard. Those who had curly-coated dogs wanted that. Those who had smooth, flat-coated dogs said that was best because burrs wouldn't tangle in the floppy ears. Never before was a dog accepted as a breed until it threw generations of uniformly true litters. Here is the first case where the cart was put before the horse.

The Boykins of Boykin Community made the society a family project. It was Kitty Beard, a Boykin descendant on her mother's side, who was the organizer and working force behind the scenes to get the society started. Records went back only to 1940. Kitty wrote letters to everyone she could find in the country who owned a Boykin and an organization was established. There were eight founders. It was veterinarian Peter McKoy who had the role of referee and kept things moving until they did write a standard for the dog. But a standard by committee had to make everyone happy, so, for example, the wording of the description of the dog's coat allows everything from a flat to a moderately curly coat of medium length, but a short straight coat is also acceptable—anything goes, even tight curly.

The society has over two thousand members, and over six thousand dogs are registered. The standard satisfies almost everyone. They're just hoping that future dogs will have a characteristic "Boykin look."

But the Boykin problems are nowhere near settled. Baynard Boykin and Whit Boykin, grandson of Alec White's friend, along with Doc McKoy, feel the main purposes of the dog should be as a hunting dog and a companion. They are firmly against the dog's being put in the show ring. When asked if they wanted the Boykin to be recognized by the American Kennel Club, all three threw up their hands and answered, "Absolutely not!" Doc explained:

The reason we do not want the society to go AKC is because we have seen hunting breeds that have become pretty as show dogs, bred for conformation, entirely lose their hunting instinct. For example, the Poodle, the Cocker Spaniel, the Irish Setter, the show English Setter, just to name four right off the top.

We want this dog to be preserved as a hunting dog. That is extremely important. We feel that form has to follow function. I don't want some fat, pigeon-toed, American Kennel Club judge who has never hunted dictating the direction of this breed.

Once the founders got the society established, they turned the control over to a fifteen-person board of directors, which is proving cumbersome. Now some of the founders are not too pleased with the way things are going and privately are sorry they gave up their leadership. The board is misinformed and confused about the whole new testing program that has been set up in this country for hunting dogs, and as the popularity of the Boykin increases, more and more nonhunters will get hold of the dog. Too high numbers is the signal to raise the red flag of danger.

Twenty or maybe forty years down the road this dog will go the way of the Cocker, Poodle, and Irish Setter, who can't hunt and find their own supper. There is only one reason this has happened to those breeds: politics. The dogs don't do this to themselves; the people ruin our working dogs. What any working breed needs to succeed, and stay a worker, is to keep working. To keep the hunting in a breed, a known gene pool of proven hunters must be available for breeding stock.

The Boykin Spaniel Society is putting itself in a box, and its dog will be the loser. It wants the dog to prove itself neither in the show ring, which is understandable, nor in the field, which is not understandable. The directors are giving lip service to wanting to keep the dog a hunter, but they are doing little about it. Lip service and desire will not a hunter make.

Already there is a major split in the society: the hunters against the nonhunters. The Carolina Boykin Spaniel Club is a separate field-test group. The Boykin society does not recognize it or its field activities. Not only should the Boykin society recognize the work of the field-test group, but it should be out organizing more field-test clubs and recording field accomplishments on the pedigrees.

The Boykin is in a critical phase of its development. It's becoming a popular little fellow, and that has always spelled trouble for a working breed.

Too many people start to own the dog who have no interest in its work. With the society only recognizing a standard for conformation, the dog's working ability will go down the drain. No dog can survive popularity in the pet market *and* keep its working skills unless specific steps are taken to ensure a gene pool of working stock.

It is important to field-test the dogs so breeding stock can be managed. There is such a national testing program in this country, called the North American Hunting Retriever Association (NAHRA). It tests a dog against a hunting standard, not through competition between dogs. The standard is written to test all categories, from dogs that are just starting to learn their job, showing native ability, to the finished master retrievers. Unless the Boykin Spaniel Society joins NAHRA or sets up its own written working, hunting standard, as it has done for conformation, the dog's future will be in jeopardy. Conformation alone is a cop-out. It's a beauty contest without demonstrating any talent—beautiful but dumb.

This dog has to do the kind of work today that it accomplished for Alec White and Whit Boykin eighty years ago. Unless a working program is initiated for breeding purposes, the Boykin will end up being just another pet.

If the board of directors of the Boykin Spaniel Society wanted to eliminate the politics in its dog game, it should answer one question and then follow up on the answer. Would Whit Boykin and Alec White set up a testing program to protect the dog's future as a hunter?

Unless the society makes a strong stand and stops making decisions by committee to satisfy everyone, the dog will be back on the stoop of the Spartanburg church. He's going to be an awfully cute fellow sitting there waiting for Sunday dinner, but he will have forgotten how to hunt.

An Educated Guess at the Boykin's Background

When all the facts are assembled, there is a good logical guess that the unknown dog that was found at the church by Alec White in Spartanburg, just after the turn of the century, was actually a lost American Water Spaniel. Did they start out as the same dog?

The American and the curly-haired Boykin spaniels are in many ways dead ringers for each other, except that the Boykin today is a little smaller and has yellow eyes and a docked tail. The American, as we have said, was a dog used by the Indians in Wisconsin. But after the Civil War, when settlers moved west, they found the dog and used it as their working retriever. However, no one outside the very small area of the Wolf River in Wisconsin knew about the dog until about 1920. By 1940 it had become so popular in the West that it was recognized by the American Kennel Club. These dates become a key factor in this search.

The year 1909 is about when Alec White found Dumpy in Spartanburg, and the same year that the physician, Dr. F. J. Pfiefer, started to develop a pure American Water Spaniel in Wisconsin. Pfiefer had known the "Indian Dog" as a boy, in 1876, but the dog had been known in his New London area of Wisconsin for generations before that.

Interestingly, the Wolf River, Wisconsin, and the Wateree River, South Carolina, had similar needs for a small hunting dog and retriever. Two small rural areas, widely separated, were simultaneously developing a dog to do similar work. But there was no way the Boykin people in South Carolina would have known in 1909 what was happening a thousand miles or more away in Wisconsin. Dumpy, the dog Alec found, was a fine water retriever and excellent hunter. Hunting and water-retrieving have to be in a dog's genes. Excelling at these isn't just luck, especially when these skills are successfully passed on to the dog's progeny.

In view of these facts, consider this question: if a western settler had brought a dog back east with him about 1908 and it got lost, no one in Spartanburg or Boykin Community would have known what it was. Could Dumpy have been a lost American Water Spaniel?

Later, when the American Water Spaniel got its first national attention, in 1940, the Boykin people thought it looked so much like their own dog that they imported it for breeding stock, according to Arden Lowndes, an old-time breeder from Camden, South Carolina. In 1943 Bolivar DeSaussure Boykin, the son-in-law of Whit, wrote to Driscoll Scanlan, who was the first president of the American Water Spaniel Club. For fifty dollars Scanlan sent two American pups to South Carolina. The bitch may not have survived. Bolivar Boykin's daughter "Pete" Rose does not remember the female but has snapshots of the male American, named Turk. He was used extensively to breed into the Boykin line. Then, in 1951, Arden Lowndes, a Yankee who retired to Camden, introduced another American Water Spaniel into his kennel. He felt his Boykins always had that American Water Spaniel look and imported one from Illinois, as he says, "to strengthen the basic Boykin breeding stock." Interestingly, he also called his import Turk.

Information today from the old-time breeders in Wisconsin substantiates this input of Americans into Boykins. From the late 1950s to the late 1960s, Joe Tryba and Father Vaughn V. Brockman were selling and shipping American Water Spaniels to the South. Their progeny were registered then as Boykins. Father Brockman tells a story of a litter born with yellow eyes. Americans have brown eyes. Being very concerned, he asked Joe Tryba about the matter. Tryba replied, "Don't worry. We can sell all the yellow-eyed pups to the Boykin breeders. All they do is dock the tail and they then have Boykins."

All the yellow-eyed Americans date back to the 1920s from a dog called Fosgate Rusty. It was a Chesapeake cross, owned by Dr. J. P. Foskett of Meridian, Ohio. Rusty was an outstanding worker and was used extensively in breeding. He had the yellow eyes of a Boykin. An earlier dog from this strain might have been the dog that got to South Carolina. But how far Rusty's lineage went back is not known, because in his background was the unrecorded Chessie cross, and that is where the line stopped.

Father Brockman did not wish to give the names of the Boykin breeders he sold American Water Spaniels to in the late 1960s. Then, he said, that business stopped. This fits the story that in the early 1970s the Boykin, according to writer Creel, almost disappeared.

Father Brockman was concerned that printing this story would make the Boykin folks angry. Then he recalled, "I shipped an American to a family in, I believe, South Carolina. Three weeks later I called to see about the pup. Their young son answered the phone, and I asked him how the pup was doing. The boy answered, 'Not too well. My father just cut his tail off.' "

Mike Creel, who became the first chronicler of the Boykin, was under the misapprehension that the Boykin Spaniel was an older breed than the American Water Spaniel. The confusing element was the 1940 date, which was when the American was recognized by the AKC and first got national attention. Creel did not realize that the American Water Spaniel had been known in the Wisconsin area since just after the Civil War. When asked, "Since the American was not known in South Carolina until after it was recognized in 1940, what chances are there that the Boykin is really an

American Water Spaniel?" Creel agreed, saying, "Chances are good. Even today they sure look alike."

After mulling it over, this writer now understands what editor John Culler meant when he said, "I don't believe there is any such thing as a Boykin Spaniel!"

The Nova Scotia Duck Tolling Retriever

It may be true that curiosity killed the cat, but that's only part of the story. It killed the ducks and geese too.

The Nova Scotia Duck Tolling Retriever entices resting ducks and geese to the shore to find out what the dog's antics are all about. With a little "assistance" from the hunter hiding on the shore, it all ends up as duck soup.

It's a fact that has been known a long time—ducks and geese can be attracted, almost mesmerized, by strange antics of a dog on the shore. It was most likely an "art" developed when a hunter watched a pair of foxes working a flock of rafted-up waterfowl. While one fox hid in the bushes, the other did the attracting. Just when this kind of hunting started is hard to say. Nondescript dogs had been used in Europe since before the invention of gunpowder to lure waterfowl into nets. The American Indian, knowing the ways of the fox, developed his own system of tolling waterfowl. Using a fox skin, with the tail extending up, strung on a line between two blinds, the Indians "danced" the "fox" back and forth across the open beach. That was only the first part of their skill; the second part was killing the bird on the water with a bow and arrow. It is said that the French fishermen who saw the Indians in Nova Scotia work their act took the idea back to France and developed a dog to do the job. Thus the world was introduced to Canard à l'Orange.

Tolling, as we know it today, certainly dates back to the early 1800s. J. S. Skinner in his book *The Dog and the Sportsman* devotes a chapter to "Toling for Ducks." (He uses the old spelling of the word, a corruption of "tolling," which comes from the Middle English word *tollen,* meaning to draw or entice.) He states that the practice started in Maryland some forty years before his book was published in 1845. He says, "Keep your dog in constant motion: and a red color is best, and a long bushy tail of great advantage."

Frank Forester in 1848 wrote in his *Field Sports,* "Red or Chestnut-colored dogs, with long bushy tails, are best for the purpose of Toling: the nearer they approach the color and appearance of a fox the better."

Henry C. Folkard, in his book *The Wildfowler,* published in London in 1864, gives a good accounting of the toller. He writes:

> There is one system of fowling practiced in America which is as curious in performance as it is interesting. It is probably one of the most remarkable methods ever invented, and approaches the nearest to the system of decoy as practiced in England of any of the arts employed by the people of a foreign country for the capture of wildfowl. The method alluded to is termed "Tol-

The Nova Scotia Duck Tolling Retriever lures the game into gun range with its antics on the shore.

ing." I am unable to trace the origin of the term, unless it simply implies death knell, for such it assuredly assumes to those birds which approach within range of the secreted sportsman. This singular proceeding is said to have been first introduced near Havre-de-Grace, in Maryland; and, according to traditional testimony, the art was accidentally discovered by a sportsman whilst patiently lying in ambush watching a paddling of wild ducks, which were a little beyond the range of his gun. Whilst in a state of doubt and anxiety as to whether they would approach near enough to be shot, he suddenly observed them raising their heads and swim towards the shore apart from his ambuscade; and whilst wondering at the cause of so strange a proceeding, his attention was directed to a fox which was skipping about on the shore, and evidently enticing the ducks to approach. This accidental discovery of so weak a point in the nature of the feathers tribe led the sportsman to turn it to advantage, and thus arose the curious art of "toling." To practice it successfully the sportsman requires simply the service of a dog, which he uses in a similar way to that of a "piper" employed at an English decoy.

For the purpose of "toling" the American sportsman erects blinds or screens on the margin of some lake, the resort of waterfowl; when any birds are in sight upon the water, he, and his dog, takes up a position behind the screen, and by throwing small bits of wood or pebbles up and down the shore, he keeps the dog in active motion so as to attract the attention of the birds, and induce them to swim towards the shore within a few yard of the screen, when, if they do, the sportsman immediately discharges his fowling piece at them and sometimes kills large numbers at a shot. The principal things to be observed are, a strict silence, and to keep the dog constantly in motion, and all the time in sight of the ducks. The animal should be encouraged to skip and bound over the rocks and stones in front of the screens, and to flourish his tail about with playful vivacity. He must never bark, for that would alarm the fowl and cause them to fly away immediately.

There seems to be no other record of that breed of tolling dog on Maryland's Eastern Shore. The scene changes to Nova Scotia. It seems that independently the idea was developed on their shores. And that dog, the Nova Scotia Duck Tolling Retriever, was seen on the Eastern Shore in the early 1900s. Some say the Nova Scotia dog originated in Maritime Canada with the Micmac Indians. It is told that Andrew McGray in 1882 watched a Micmac Indian throwing sticks on the beach for his foxlike dog to fetch. That action lured a flock of geese to the Indian's gun. Fascinated by this, McGray traded for the dog, which was said to be a crossbred fox dog.

The idea of a fox dog has been part of the myth, but we know now that

that is not genetically possible. Another story states that in 1860, one James Allen created the tolling dog by crossing a Flat-Coated Retriever, which he had bought from a captain of a Yarmouth schooner, with a Labrador-type dog. The puppies were bred to a spaniel and those pups bred to an Irish Setter. True or false is anyone's guess. And what is in the dog is anyone's guess too. What most likely happened, as with so many other breeds, is that the locals who had dogs that worked well used them for breeding. Many believe now there is Chesapeake, Spitz, Collie, and possibly Beagle and Springer Spaniel blood in the Toller.

The Nova Scotia Toller is a thirty- to fifty-pound, compact, red dog with a great plumed brush tail like a fox's. A white marking on the tail is preferred, and there is usually a white blaze on his face, chest, and feet. The Toller is a sensitive dog and takes readily to training.

Today the names of the Nova Scotia Duck Tolling Retriever and Avery Nickerson are almost synonymous. The dog was developed in the Little River Area near Yarmouth. For forty years Nickerson has had his Harbour Light Kennel only a few miles from the Little River.

There were others before Nickerson who were proponents of the Toller. Eddie Kenny, an old man when he sold Avery his first dog in 1945, always had a yard full of them. When asked where he thought they came from, he said he didn't know. He had known them all his life because his grandfather always had "Little River Duck Dogs." Nickerson said that the man who knew most about using the Toller was Dick Crowell. He taught Nickerson, as a young man, the fine points of the art of tolling.

The man who almost gets lost in the story of the Toller is Henry Albert Patterson Smith, a most flamboyant character who certainly was the first man to promote the dog. He was the sheriff of Digby County, president of the Nova Scotia Guides Association, ornithologist, accomplished salmon fisherman, and a writer for *Forest and Stream,* the forerunner of America's *Field and Stream.* He wrote early in this century and produced thirteen manuscripts on the tolling dogs.

> With nose as true as a pointer's, with sight as keen as the greyhound's, with endurance as great as the foxhound's, with courage equaling the bulldog's, with disposition as playful as the spaniel's, with coat as dense as the otter's, . . . his colour is fox-red from the end of his nose to the tip of his bushy tail, save a white dash on his broad chest, and in some specimens a white blaze in

the face. The above is a fair description of the tolling dog, whose equal as a duck dog the writer has yet to meet. . . .

In Nova Scotia our best game ducks are blacks and scaup, and both birds will toll to the antics of this dog.

The bufflehead and the merganser ducks will also toll, but the goldeneye will jump into the air at the sight of him, as if a gun were discharged in their midst. Sea ducks and coot seem to take no notice of the dog. But many a fat black duck has paid the penalty of his curiosity.

From a blind built on the beach out of old lobster pots draped with seaweed, Smith would repeatedly toss a hard rubber ball along the beach, and his tolling dog, Buff, would chase after it. Buff's antics as he picked up the ball and brought it back to the blind would draw a flock of curious black ducks in to the shore near the blind where Smith and his companion waited.

I nod and two pair of 12-bore barrels poke out above the fringe of seaweed of the blind. As we raise to shoot, Buff peeks over the blind beside me with a whimper and stiffened sinews waiting the report. Both shots snap out as one

The long white-tipped tail of the Nova Scotia Duck Tolling Retriever acts like a flag to get the ducks' attention.

and into the air seven terrified birds spring straight up, three of their members falling to our second barrels. There are two cripples.

Buff by this time has almost reached the nearest drifting victims. Watch him swim! . . . No need to tell him to retrieve, dropping his birds on the sand he plunges in again and again until the eighth and last duck is safely recovered.

What Is the Canadian Tolling Retriever's Future?

Avery Nickerson insists the Toller is a good upland hunter besides doing a good job on ducks. But I am not sure that added feature is going to help the dog. There are many proven flushing and pointing dogs available to the hunter. It just does not seem likely that the hunter will add the Toller to his list of choices in spite of the fact that those who use the dog claim he is a top-flight retriever.

Although the Canadian Kennel Club recognized the Nova Scotia Duck Tolling Retriever as a breed in 1945, that can only complicate the picture. For their part they have turned the Toller into a show dog. This, as we know, has always spelled trouble for a working breed because too many of those who show don't work their dogs.

Although the dog has never been considered as a field-trial dog, there was much talk when NAHRA started about getting the Toller into the field-working program. Unfortunately for the dog not much has happened. If the Toller is good enough to make it in this testing program, the hunter would certainly take note. But the same hunter takes note that the Nova Scotia Duck Tolling Retriever is not being trained or showing up at NAHRA events.

Actually, here is a grand dog that is being caught up in our modern society. Tolling takes large open areas and strung-out shorelines to work the ducks. Such areas for duck hunting have practically ceased to exist. The outboard motor and the vacation and weekend homes on so much of our open water shores have changed our hunting geography. There are not very many places left to give the tolling retriever a chance to do its job. The popularity of duck hunting itself hinders this dog. Its job calls for isolation, and duck hunters in a blind a few hundred yards down the shore from where a Toller is working won't help matters. Too much is going on to interrupt the concentration of the ducks as the foxlike dog does its work on shore. In spite of the dog's fine personality, if it does not become popular before the social and environmental changes become complete, the Nova Scotia Duck Tolling Retriever will only be a curiosity in the future.

The Saddest Retriever of Them All— the Poodle

As we saw in Chapter 3, the Poodle may have played an important role in the earliest days of waterfowl hunting in Britain. It's very possible that this dog that came from central Europe, and then into England by way of France, could have been the basis of much retriever breeding before the 1800s.

Talk to average Poodle breeders in America today, and somehow they all can tell you, from what they have read, that the Poodle is a hunting dog, a retriever, and that's all they know about it.

If this poor dog could tell its own story, it would be a sad tale indeed. In 1890 only one Poodle was registered in the United States. Within sixty years, it had become the most popular dog in the country, and it held that place for twenty-three years, a record that may never be broken. This kind of popularity in the pet and show world will ruin the "work" in any breed. It was the Cocker Spaniel that beat the Poodle out for first place in popularity in 1983, and now the Cocker is in the same situation—it can't hunt either.

Although through the earlier part of this century the Poodle was used as a hunter in central Europe, the big, standard Poodle was never really given a chance in America to be a worker. Sadly, the show people have made him into a clown. They have modified the hunting cut with pom-poms and ribbons, and it is not a happy sight to see this once noble hunter, who is still extremely intelligent, transformed into a sissy prancing around the show ring.

There were two groups that tried to save the Poodle from that embarrassment, but it seems that neither was completely successful. The Green-

The Poodle was most likely one of the first retrieving dogs in Britain. *(Courtesy Charles Le Boutillier, Jr.)*

Some forty years ago Martha Covington was successfully training Poodles for the field. *(Courtesy Charles Le Boutillier, Jr.)*

spring Poodle Club in the early 1950s tried to train and work standard Poodles for retrieving. According to Charles Le Boutillier, they were very successful in proving that the dogs could do the work. Le Boutillier, now in his mid-eighties, feels that they were not too successful in their overall objective because the Poodle people were not interested in undertaking the amount of work it took to train the dogs and because not every dog was potentially a good worker. It would take breeding for the work, and that would be a long, complicated process. Le Boutillier feels the Poodle today is not as smart as it was, as a result of breeding for the show ring.

The other group was composed of two duck and goose hunters of the Eastern Shore of Maryland: Dorman Covington and his wife, Martha, who was a professional retriever trainer, back in 1958 were using large Royal Standard Poodles in their hunting blinds. They trained the dogs exactly the same way as Labradors and often worked them together. They took to the work with great enthusiasm. But even with publicity in *Sports Illustrated* magazine, the whole project just faded away.

There is a great quote from Joe May, a devoted hunter and an officer of the James River Retriever Club in Virginia: "About ten years ago a lady showed up with two of those dogs at one of our retriever working sessions. One white and the other black. All I know is that everybody laughed at those dogs when she showed up and nobody was laughing when she left."

But the Poodle never had a chance in America. It was an image problem. The name Poodle comes from the German *Pudel* meaning "water splasher." In America Poodles were only known to splash around in *eau de cologne,* not in a wet, swampy, duck marsh.

5

Retrieving on the American Scene

The retriever era didn't fully arrive in America until the Depression years of the 1930s. The Labrador brought it on, and it got its impetus from the socially prominent, a decade earlier, in the roaring twenties.

Small isolated areas such as the Eastern Shore of Maryland, where waterfowl sport hunting was the major shooting game, had their Chesapeake Bay Retrievers well established by the latter part of the last century. The same was true in Wisconsin, where they had the American Water Spaniel. In these cases, and the Boykin should be included, the numbers were relatively small. This was the time when the English Setter reigned as king of the hunting dogs in this country and the Pointer was a close second. It most likely would have stayed that way, with the upland dogs doing the big job in a country like ours, with lots of land, and the relatively few retrievers doing their specialized job on the waterfowl flyways. This was changed by a small isolated group who were a true product of those roaring twenties. They were the socially prominent sportsmen located in the Tuxedo section of New York, about fifty miles up the Hudson from New York City. This was the place where the wealthy lived and played. This was the time when great

128

The British benefactors of the Labrador were the aristocracy. In America it was the wealthy and socially prominent. Here Marshall Field *(left)* talks to his trainer, Douglas Marshall.

fortunes were accumulated, the time of the jazz era, the flapper, the Charleston, F. Scott Fitzgerald, the speakeasy, and good Scotch whiskey.

After World War I, the socially elite, wealthy Americans were fascinated by European royalty, titles, and the social order of England and Scotland. The Victorian era, which tolerated no invasion by outsiders, was coming to an end, and our wealthy could "buy" their way into the British society. The "in" thing was to have British aristocracy as one's friends, and nothing could be more elegant than an invitation to shoot driven pheasant in Yorkshire or driven grouse on the Scottish moors. The "new" Americans enjoyed castle living and emulated their British friends by building castles of their own. It was a time when American money did anything it desired.

There was no sport in America that compared to the elegance of the Scottish driven shoot with all its social grandeur. The wealthy Americans set out and imported the whole shebang, truly, lock, stock, and barrel. Not only did they buy the best of British guns (lock, stock, and barrel), but they imported the fine British country casual living even down to the shooting clothes. They brought over and established Scottish gamekeepers on their New York estates, and with them came the fine Labradors from the best British working kennels. A dozen or so families turned their estates into shooting preserves, and the keepers raised 100,000 game birds a year. They had parties that were more like Hollywood productions. Fine chauffeured limousines brought the ladies and gentlemen to the country estates for three- or four-day "weekend" shoots.

Between shooting events, elegantly dressed ladies and men in sporting tweeds luncheoned on the lawn. It was truly the time of Gatsby, with formal dinner parties and dancing in the evening. The gamekeepers were supplied with Scotch and made their own music, but as in British tradition the two groups never mixed.

Since both the land on the American estates and the game available were unlike those of Great Britain, the gamekeepers had to simulate the British conditions. Instead of armies of beaters to gather and flush the game over the guns, they improvised with an ingenious system of tower shoots. This was best accomplished by placing a dozen or so guns at stations in roughly a three-hundred-yard circle around a high piece of land, such as a wooded mound. Then hundreds or even a thousand pheasants would be released in singles or pairs from the central place on the high ground to fly over the guns. Such shooting is very sporty, and the "game" is still played in some of our exclusive shooting clubs.

Averell Harriman was the first to bring a Scottish gamekeeper, Tom Briggs, to this country. On his Harriman, New York, estate, situated on a mountaintop, young ducks were trained, first to walk, and then, when mature, to fly from a hilltop (where they were fed) to a lake below. After their daily swim, they would go back to the hilltop to eat and rest. Once the ducks had been trained and were old enough to be strong fliers, the guns were put at butts to intercept them on their flight down to the lake. It was excellent pass shooting.

Dressed in their tweed Norfolk jackets and knickers, the Americans also simulated the British walk-up shooting. The English do it in beet fields, which we did not have. The ingenious Americans made it into a "Cecil B. de Mille production." As the line of guns and dog handlers walked through a field, boys in pits threw pheasants at the oncoming, walking line. The sport for the ladies and gentlemen was the shooting. Gillies carried the shot birds, and the keepers saw to it that it happened like clockwork. The Labs, working

Averell Harriman was the first to import a Scottish gamekeeper, Tom Briggs, who was an expert on breeding and training.

Lord Knutsford founded the Labrador Club of England in 1916.

for the keepers, made the retrieves as part of the "authentic" scenario. It all had the theatricality of a set in an old-fashioned war movie, rather than a hunting field. To recover the birds missed by the shooting parties, the Labs were then used as flushing dogs, to quarter the fields and "clean up" the area, something the British never did.

Some of the most elegant events were held on the eight-thousand-acre Glenmere Court estate owned by Robert Goelet of Chester, New York. It wasn't long before the new game spread to the wealthy families of Long Island. Mr. and Mrs. Marshall Field became big supporters of the Labrador. The Morgans, Belmont, Carlisles, Lords, Laurences, and Elys were all names found in the social register. It was about a dozen or so families that started playing the new game.

But the game ended almost as abruptly as it started. The October 1929 stock market crash brought an end to these lavish "Hollywood" productions. As one looks back, this put the Labrador in a very precarious position. The dog was in no way the main focus of these shoots. The whole game was a synthetic reproduction where the gamekeepers, clothes, fine guns, birds, and dogs were the props for the actors. The dog was there only to make the game as authentic as possible and was the gamekeeper's responsibility. As yet in America no one was "looking out" for the Lab. With the market crash, and people jumping out of windows, the Lab could have gone the way of the flapper.

The English by this time had taken an important step for their dog. The Labrador Retriever Club had been started in 1916 by Lord Knutsford and Lorna, Countess Howe. Although disaster hit the whole dog world in England during World War I, by the 1920s it was reestablished and the Labrador had become very popular. There was no such organization in America looking out for our Labs. Luckily, however, there was a second development in this wealthy arena. Private clubs were established that literally put the Labrador "on hold" until the general hunting population was educated to the ways of this retriever and saw its real usefulness. Here is how that story unwinds.

The Labrador Saved Again by a Fluke

As you will recall, the third earl of Malmesbury's kennel was in jeopardy. At that time the Lab's future was saved by a fluke. It was the chance meeting, while duck hunting, of Lord Malmesbury and the duke of Buccleuch and Lord Home on the south coast of England. That meeting continued the established line of dogs at Heron Court through the Buccleuch kennels in Scotland, and the dogs were successfully brought into the twentieth century.

Again, this time, in 1930 the Lab's future in the United States wasn't worth much more than some of the stocks on Wall Street. The hunter in America had no contact with this dog, as the elegant weekend shooting parties and shooting clubs were very private and exclusive. But even if the hunter could have seen this world, just on the face of things, the dog added nothing that the hunter didn't already have. His upland dogs were the English Setter and the Pointer, and his waterfowl dog was the Chessie. It comes as news to a lot of people, but the Labrador at that point was not a waterfowler's dog. Those skills came a few years later. The Labrador was a land retriever. Since the American hunter didn't play the English game, what good was a dog that only walked at heel while the other dogs worked finding the game? The Lab retrieved the game only when it was down. It made more sense for the American hunter to have a second pointing dog who could find game and also retrieve, giving him another working dog to help fill the pot. There was no real need for the Labrador in the American hunting scene. Since the average hunter knew little or nothing about the dog, the Lab could have faded away. With the Depression affecting every segment of our society, including the elegant private shooting at which the dog was imported to perform, the Lab had a questionable future.

The Lab Is Saved

Three things happened that saved the dog. First, with the phasing out of the elaborate country weekend house parties that were in the Victorian tradition, private shooting clubs took their place. The Blooming Grove Club in Pennsylvania and Wyandanche Club on Long Island were two of the early ones, and they were very exclusive. They produced the same kind of sport as the exclusive private parties.

Second, these clubs also imported the Scottish gamekeepers. The whole concept of this shooting game depended on the gamekeeper. He knew how to raise the birds, care for the grounds, run the shooting events, and train the dogs. With more gamekeepers coming to America, there were more dogs. By the early 1930s there was quite a community of gamekeepers in America, and they became a "holding pen" for their dog, whose popularity would soon explode on the American scene.

Another thing that helped save the Lab from oblivion in the United States was the English tradition of retriever trials. Jim Cowie, one of the early keepers, hired by Tom Briggs on the Harriman estate, said that it might

Jim Cowie, an imported Scottish gamekeeper, thought that field trials got started in the United States because the gamekeepers were homesick. Jim spent his whole life with retrievers, both in the show ring and in the field. *(Author Photo)*

have been homesickness that led to the idea of having a field event for the dogs. At home, in Scotland, field trials had become a major part of the keepers' lives. It was their off-season sport and a focus of their social life.

There is very little documentation on just how the first field trial was set up. We do know that the whole social life of the keepers evolved around their own little community in America. They did the same work, had the same income, same social status, came from the same mother country, had the same customs, so it is obvious that they were a close-knit group. One thing they did as a group on a regular basis was to get together to help one another train their dogs. The obvious outgrowth of that was the desire to have a field trial.

Jim Cowie recalled that the owners were not too pleased by the idea and in fact agreed to it only to humor the gamekeepers. Since the keepers had already been getting together on a regular basis, this event had to be more than an informal affair. This meant running the trial through the sponsorship of the American Kennel Club. To do this, the Labrador Retriever Club had to be formed. Very little seems to be documented about how this was done and how the AKC recognized the new Labrador breed club and accepted the dog as a recognized breed so quickly. The usual practice is that it takes years and much paperwork to get a dog accepted by the AKC. Possibly even the AKC could not challenge this distinguished list of officers and members: Mrs. Marshall Field, of New York, Chicago, and Huntington, Long Island, president; Mr. Robert Goelet and Mr. Frank B. Lord, vice-presidents; and Wilton Loyd-Smith, secretary-treasurer. The membership list of the club was just more names from the "register." It is thought that Frank B. Lord, a prominent New York attorney, was the prime mover.

When it came time to make the specific plans for the first trial, George F. Foley, the AKC's dog show organizer, of Philadelphia, was called in.

That first trial was held on December 21, 1931, at Goelet's Glenmere Court estate in Chester, New York. The judges were David Wagstaff and Dr. Samuel Milbank, men of outstanding reputations not only with retrievers but with pointing dogs as well. Both Mr. and Mrs. Marshall Field ran their dogs along with Douglas Marshall, their gamekeeper and trainer. Henry Root Stern, H. F. Guggenheim, Paul Hammond, Robert G. McKay, and Robert Goelet were among the distinguished handlers in the Open All-Age sixteen-dog stake.

Although the catalogue for the trial states on its cover that the event was held under the rules of the American Kennel Club and the Labrador Retriever Club, these rules have never been found. The trial was set up as the same game the gamekeepers played at home in Scotland. There were no specific tests. The dog work came naturally from the shooting situations. Freeman Lloyd, the most important dog writer of the day, gave a full account of the event in the January 2, 1932, issue of *Popular Dogs*.

> At this meeting the birds were walked up: that is to say, the advancing line of three guns, gun attendants, the two handlers with dogs at heel, and beaters advanced in line with a gun right center and left. Behind strode the gallery, among whom were many women of much social distinction and affluence.
>
> The first and second prizes in the Open All-Age Stake were won by Mrs.

Marshall Field's Carl of Boghurst and Odds On. Carl was handled by Mrs. Field and Odds On taken in hand by the head of the house. . . .

A large house party was entertained at The Court, while the banquet provided for the handlers, beaters and others at the American House Hotel proved a fine harbinger of the good things of Christmastide. And the catering of the bountiful Mrs. Smyth, lady of the old-time Inn in the far famed valley, was as generous as it was good.

It sounds as though writer Lloyd made it to the handlers' party and not to the house party at The Court. This was also true in Britain; through the nineteenth century, the English sporting writer was never accepted in the aristocratic circles, and that is why he was so poorly informed.

Those were the good old days, when the shooting sports had a touch of elegance. Today you don't get a cup of coffee at a trial. One very important thing happened at this event. What started as an event to humor the gamekeepers ended as a genuine interest in the dogs by the owners. The game of retriever field trialing caught on and was off to an auspicious start. It was a historic occasion but not as important for the future of the Labrador as the next series of events.

That first retriever trial set the scene for the Chesapeake Bay Retriever Club to hold its first field trial. That event proved to be a disaster for the Labrador because the tests were all water work and the Labs were field dogs. The Labs were beaten badly. But it so happened that this "disaster" turned out to be the lucky fluke that cemented the future for the Labrador in the United States. As Jim Cowie remembered it, the Labradors and their trainers went home with their tails between their legs. A year was spent retraining the dogs into water retrievers. Being great natural swimmers, they came back the following year and beat the Chessie at its own game.

That message quickly reached the average hunter. Here was a first-rate upland dog with a great hunting nose who could also beat the Chessie in water work. He was easy to train and had the disposition of a baby-sitter. Almost overnight, the great worker, the Chessie, the hardheaded, one-man dog, whose disposition at times was questionable, was replaced in the duck blinds by the Labrador. The Labrador's future was secure. And the game of field trialing was here to stay—but as a wealthy man's game.

The 1930s brought an interesting development to the retriever game. In some ways, it was separated from actual hunting, and the trial became a game unto itself. Most of the participants were sporting and gunning people, but in some ways it was like horseracing. The owners never did the riding but only came out to see their "horseflesh" perform.

Retriever clubs sprang up all over the country, from coast to coast. It was still a rich man's sport. The Scottish gamekeepers changed professions and now became dog trainers. Some trainers went to work for a private family and ran their kennels, and some trainers had their own kennel and took on a number of clients.

It was a most interesting period of development, but there are very few records of exactly how the game changed and developed from the British system the gamekeepers introduced. The English system of field trials allows twenty-four dogs to participate in a two-day event, twelve dogs in a one-day event. Those numbers never seemed to have been recorded or even referred to in the American events. In Britain, if the entry of dogs exceeded twenty-four or twelve, according to the event, the dogs were picked by lottery. Those first trials in America never had the problem of too many dogs to run in one day. But the sport grew, and the American Kennel Club would not allow the lottery system. They claimed that all dogs that paid the entrance fee and were in good standing with the AKC should run. That presented a problem. Running the dogs as walk-ups, in the British tradition, didn't allow more than twelve dogs a day to be handled before dark.

We know from an interview with Averell Harriman (*The Labrador Retriever . . . The History . . . The People,* p. 83) that in 1934 the system used in trials was still the British walk-up. In 1935 E. F. Warner, publisher of *Field and Stream* magazine, donated a trophy to be awarded to the "Outstanding Retriever of the Year." Interestingly, the game was still so exclusive that there is no record of the award. But the trophy indicates the growing popularity of the new sport.

We know from Jasper Briggs, Tom Briggs's son, who followed in his father's footsteps and became a trainer on the Harriman estate, and from Jim Cowie that the Scottish trainers got together with their dogs and held training sessions. (Their names should not be lost in time: Billy Gladwin trained for Mrs. Moffatt; Jack Monroe and Colin Macfarlane for Robert Goelet; Leon Bond for Dr. Milbank; Ernest Wells for Dave Wagstaff; Russ Murdock for Gould Remick; Laurence McQueen for W. K. Dick; and, as independents, Alex Cummings, Martin Hogan, and his sons James and Francis.)

Because birds were not as abundant here, these men developed a system for their training sessions in America that was not needed in Scotland. It proved to be fast and efficient, and it cost less. It was simple: instead of taking the dogs to the game, they brought the game to the dog. Instead of walking the dog through the cover until game was found, shot, and then retrieved, they brought the dog to a point and sat it down. Fifty yards away, or at whatever distance they wanted to use, a bird was thrown into the air and when it landed the dog was sent for the retrieve. The bird could be a live runner, a shot dead bird, or a crippled bird. This way ten dogs could be trained on birds in the same time it took one dog to get a retrieve in the walk-up method, and you didn't need as many people.

As the sport of field trials became popular, a system had to be devised to handle more than the British twelve dogs a day. The answer was to use the Scottish trainers' system of bringing the game birds to the dogs. Exactly when this was decided, and by whom, is not known, but by 1937 it was being done this way all over the country. It opened up the sport so that today we can run a hundred dogs a day if need be.

One of the gamekeepers who came to this country and left an important mark in the retriever game as we know it today was Dave Elliot.

When Jay F. Carlisle of Long Island decided in 1934 to get into the sport of Labradors and field trials, he wrote to his friend Lorna Countess Howe chairman of the Labrador Retriever Club of England, and asked that she recommend a young trainer. She did. Dave Elliot went to America.

Dave, a feisty Scotsman, recalled her as a wonderful woman if you knew how to keep your place. He came from a line of several generations of gamekeepers. At seventeen he was training retrievers on the Montrose estate in Scotland. When he came to America, he had some new ideas about how the dogs should work. In his early days in Scotland, he was fascinated by the work being done there in training sheepdogs to herd and felt that these trainers' handling techniques could be very useful in retriever work.

Dave was not the first to recognize this, but he was the one who made it part of retriever work. In 1911 Archibald Buttler, the owner and handler of a very famous dog, Peter of Faskally, won the first International Gundog League Championship by using a system based on methods for the training of sheepdogs, namely hand signals and whistles. His success was so outstanding that others tried his method, but they all failed. Buttler was considered an unreal sort of genius with dogs, and his system was forgotten. It wasn't tried again until twenty-five years later, when Elliot came up, on his own, with the same system. When Buttler's work was pointed out to Dave, he was completely unaware of it. It was truly his system.

The Americans were not ready for dog handling. If one of Dave's dogs missed the mark of a downed bird, he would stop it by whistle. The dog would turn, sit, and wait for a hand signal, then follow the signal to the bird and make the retrieve. Although Dave's dogs did outstanding work, the judges just didn't know how to score them. His dogs would place, but were not given the win. Dave stuck to his guns and continued to handle his dogs when the situation called for it. Then one day it all fell into place.

A twinkle came to Dave's eye as he told this story shortly before he went to "trainer's heaven." He sparkled and talked so fast in his Scottish burr that I had a hard time understanding him.

Jay Carlisle *(left),* who brought Dave Elliot to America, watches a field event with Charles Lawrence.

Dave Elliot did more to change and advance field trials in this country than any other one person. He is actually the father of dog handling by whistle and hand signals. *(Author Photo)*

Dave explained the test that changed things in dog training. It was a double water retrieve on a very windy day. In a wide bay, guns in a boat shot a bird a good distance from shore, having it land in the open water. A second set of guns dropped a bird in the decoys in front of the blind. All the dogs did the job the same way. They first retrieved the bird in the decoys. But by the time they accomplished that and then went for the long retrieve, the wind had drifted the bird away. The dogs went to the spot where the bird had splashed and then continued on out into the open water looking for it. Trouble loomed when the dogs hit the fast current in the open channel. The dogs were in jeopardy because they could not be handled and brought back out of danger if need be. One dog had to be chased down by boat.

All the handlers knew that a retriever by natural instinct will retrieve the last bird down first. That is how all the dogs had been doing the work. They went for the short, second bird down in the decoys first. Dave, seeing the time problem of the drifting long bird, reversed the order of retrieves. By handling he sent his dog to the long bird before it had time to drift off. The second retrieve in the decoys was simple; it would have stayed there indefinitely. This episode not only won the day for Dave, but proved the usefulness of handling.

Up until this time, especially for water blinds, if a dog did not see the

Dave Elliot in the early 1930s accepting delivery of a pheasant from Drinkstone Pons, one of the many field champions he made.

fall of a bird, it was gotten to a specific point by throwing a stone or some other object. The dog would swim to the splash. Once the dog got that far, another stone was thrown farther. A "three stoner" was considered a long blind retrieve—if the handler had a strong throwing arm. Following the splashes, the dog was gotten into the area of the bird's scent; then it could make the retrieve. In 1937, Dave was on a committee that changed the rule, and "stoner" retrieves were no longer allowed. Dave, by stubbornly sticking it out, had introduced a technique for true blind retrieves.

The "Face" of the Game Changes

There were two factors that had an important impact on the retriever field-trial game. There is no written record, but 1937 was the year that changed the face of retriever work. The first factor was bringing the game to the dog, as introduced by the Scottish trainers, and the second was the controls necessary for the handling of the dog to follow directions, as demonstrated by Dave Elliot. The first technique brought about double and triple retrieves to test the dog's memory, and the second was a test of absolute obedience. True blind retrieves could be performed. Now the game of retriever field trials was off and running, and it has never stopped. As we shall see, as the dogs got better and better, the judges made tests that were harder and harder, only to find the dogs still getting better and better. That cycle has never ended.

What this did was to eliminate the upland flushing work that the Goldens and Labs were so good at, and also to cut out the trailing of a crippled bird, which was the basis and main emphasis of the English field trials. The Americans started a new game that fulfilled their need to take care of the large entries.

Slowly the game was weaned away from the British game, but it took many years. In the middle 1930s, *staunchness* (don't move until commanded to do so) was still one of the most important ingredients in the game, and judges would throw breaking tests at the dogs through most of the series, to see if the dog would "break" to make the retrieve before it was commanded to do so. If a dog as much as stood up when the birds were released, that was a break; it was out. Creeping on line was a major sin, and the dog would be retired from the competition. This staunchness was a hangover from the British shoots of the Victorian era, when a dog was handled by a gillie and its whining or movement might interfere with the shooter's concentration.

Tests then were relatively simple compared to today's standards, and breaking was an easy way of testing and eliminating dogs. It would not be unusual for a judge to hold back the order to the handler to send his dog for a retrieve, making the dog wait if the judge even thought it might break.

Although breaking tests are still used in trials, they are usually used only in the early series. A good judge hates to lose one of his best dogs on such an unimportant part of the game. A standing dog, a creeper, or a *controlled break* (where the dog is immediately stopped), is possibly a mark-down in the judge's book but not a throw-out.

Today we have *honoring* as part of the testing. While one dog works, the other sits by and must not break or interfere with the working dog. In the AKC-licensed trials, we have eliminated the real value of the test. Today the honoring dog, who has usually just run the test and has the "steam" run out of him, only honors and watches the *falls* (birds shot or thrown) for the working dog. As soon as the working dog is sent to make the first retrieve, the honoring dog is excused and taken off line. In those early days, there might be as many as six dogs sitting in a row, honoring all at the same time. Neither the dog nor the handler would know which dog would be called on to make the retrieve. The judges would then pick one of the dogs to go.

Hunting out a crippled bird and marking a fall were the basic early testing of the retrievers. Water tests were usually short, through decoys and out into open water, rather simple stuff. But sometimes live, shackled decoys were used. I think it would be a tough job today to get a dog to swim through live birds to retrieve a dead one.

Early on, when handling first became part of the testing, the judges didn't understand how to deal with this. Usually the last series in a trial was a handling test. The judges would give the dogs about a fifty-yard blind retrieve down a dirt road. If the dog stopped on whistle (and it might take a few tries) and if it more or less followed the hand signal, and stumbled on the bird, it passed the test.

In the 1930s, the marked birds were usually thrown or shot (and the judges hoped they were only winged) into very heavy cover where you couldn't even see your dog. The dog was on its own to find the bird or fail. In the early 1940s, this changed. Field trials became a more democratic game as far as the rules were concerned. We had already seen the number of dogs entered go from the British system of twenty-four in a two-day event to any number wishing to run in the American trials. In the 1940s, the element of luck was removed from the English game by the ruling that every dog should have the exact same test. This eliminated the use in tests of running and crippled birds, and for all practical purposes, of tall cover in which you could not see your dog.

It was Paul Bakewell, the amateur handler from Ohio, who learned to take advantage of the new rules. He trained his dogs to be surefire handlers. He figured that he could remember the marks better than his dog, so he sent it to the area and, with a quick, almost foolproof system, handled the dog to the mark. This impressed the judges and seemed to be a new purpose for handling, and it became the fad. Charlie Morgan, one of the best pros of this period, said that during the end of the 1930s you almost went out of your way to impress the judges by proving the dog could handle. Of course in a licensed trial today if you handle on a marked retrieve, where the dog sees the fall, you almost might just as well pick your dog up and go home.

During the 1940s, a new fad took hold. It was the side cast, or over. Judges were impressed with dogs that would take a long cast around a bush or a tree and hold that line to the side for a good distance. This was done by having the dog first sent to a spot, a bush, or a tree, stopping it there, then sending the dog on its side cast. Today the side cast is not taught to the same extent to the field-trial dog. The reason is that if a dog is so far off course that a long side cast is needed to get it to a mark or a blind, the dog would automatically be out of the running for being so far off the direct line to the bird. Today you give an Open class dog an over, a cast to the side, and it will go to the side in the direction of the signal a short distance; then it will turn back away from the handler (this is known as *scalloping*). Today, the over command, or side cast, has really become a correction for the direct line back to the bird.

In the 1950s, the emphasis shifted to the line. The dog, sitting at the handler's side, was given a direction signal with the hand in front of its eyes. It was supposed to take that "line" and go as straight as an arrow, across hill and dale and not stop, even if it smelled game, until it heard the whistle. This was the final "act" that changed field trials from a hunter's game to an absolutely-perfect-obedience game and a game unto itself.

As the dogs and handlers learned the lining game, it soon was done with great precision. Trainer Cotton Pershall and a dog named King Buck, owned by John Olin, took the art of lining to its ultimate. Those who knew the dog said he couldn't mark a full-grown eagle if it was thrown, but he could sure take a line and run it straight to "Philadelphia." The dog was a master on the blind retrieve. If Cotton set him up correctly and pointed him right,

Cotton Pershall training King Buck. Those who saw the two Nationals they won say King Buck was the best handling dog ever. *(Courtesy of Cotton Pershall)*

King Buck would nail the blind. Cotton, knowing the dog could not mark, treated even a marked bird as a blind. Buck didn't even have to see the bird fall, and Cotton would set him up and line him to the area, and the King's nose did the rest. This skill became worth two National Championships, in 1952 and 1953.

The lining game started as just another of the judges' fads, but it was at a time when field trials had really matured and there were many excellent trainers and handlers in the game. An unwritten three-way challenge seemed to emerge among the judges, dogs, and handlers. We started to see some excellent dogs appear on the scene. The line seemed to be just what the judges needed to put the dogs to the ultimate test. As the judges took on the attitude of "Okay, let's see you do this one!" the handlers trained their dogs to do "this one." The dogs learned it and were ready. The judges then had to concoct harder tests. It became a cycle between judges and dogs, and the dog always came out on top. In the East it started with *channel blinds*. This meant that the dog had to swim a line down the center of a narrow body of water and never touch land until it reached the end of the channel. Of course it would have been faster to run the bank and shorten the swimming time and get the bird back to the handler fast. But that wasn't the game the judges wanted. Hunting was no longer a factor in the tests. Almost unbelievable feats of courage and obedience were being produced as everyday events.

Lining took on a different form in the West. The eastern judge came up with the channel blind, and the western judge came up with the *angle entry*. Think of it this way: when you dive into a swimming pool, the usual approach is to walk up to the edge and face the center of the pool and go in head first. We might call this squaring the angle entry because the diver goes in at ninety degrees to the edge of the pool. A dog will usually do the same thing. It seems to be natural. The angle entry is just what its name implies. It started off with the dog's being some running distance from the water's edge. The line the dog is given by the handler is at an angle into the water. The dog is supposed to take the handler's line, run to the water, dive in at that same angle, and swim continuing that line in the water until it is given a correction cast to put it on the exact line to the blind.

It is easy to see what has happened over a period of time as the judging ideas of the East and the West gradually met. The judges' alternatives became endless. Although the AKC rules state that the tests should simulate hunting conditions, judges and contestants alike gave the rule lip service but ignored it in the field. Actually, many of the field-trial contestants did not know much about hunting conditions, because they weren't hunters.

Minor innovations and fads continued. Triples started out with wide separation between the birds. Gradually, the angles were reduced, and the three birds became tighter and tighter. This called for precision marking.

A

B

The dog is given a line by the hand over its head. The dog runs that line until the handler wants to make a correction. The dog is stopped by whistle. In AKC-licensed field trials, the distance can be up to three hundred yards. The handler wears a white jacket so the dog can see him.

The dog is being given a cast to the side. The precision is amazing. A handler could have a dog sit on a handkerchief at two hundred yards.

Diversion birds were added to the marking mix to try to make the dog forget the original marks. Judges must have lain awake at night figuring out the next step in "Okay, let's see you do this one!" The three-way challenge progressed, with the dogs always managing to keep up. There was only one way left for a new major fad to go, and that was distances.

The distances of the marks and the unbelievable distances of the blinds

C   D

A "quarter back" signal is given, and when that correction has been made, a straight back (as in picture D) is given. The dog is so well trained that when it stops on whistle, turns and sits facing the handler to find out its next move; if it is a straight back cast it will turn in the direction of whichever hand is up. In picture D the dog would turn to its left to go back away from the handler. *(Author Photos)*

forced some handlers with eye problems to come to line with binoculars. Those first, early fifty-yard blinds, in which the dog more or less displayed control, were over. Today's field-trial dogs are so good that if one makes a false move or slips a whistle (responds wrongly), it has as much as put itself out of the competition. At times distances and conditions are such that a judge has to ask himself if the dog could hear the whistle over the sound of the wind and noise of the water. Those on the outside, such as hunters and waterfowlers watching today's events, call such retrieving work ridiculous and useless for the hunter. There is no reason for him to spend the kind of money it takes to have a dog so highly trained. Those who play the field-trial game marvel at it and enjoy the tough competition, and rightly so.

What has this done for the dog? There is no doubt that retrievers of this caliber are trained to be one of the three most sophisticated animals in the world, and this writer does not know what the other two are.

As Neil Armstrong landed on the moon one field trialer was heard asking, "I wonder what effect the space age will have on our dogs?" We shall see the answer to that shortly.

A Look at the Record

A random look at the *Retriever Field Trial News* records of the National Championships in 1947, then in 1967, and then in 1987, will tell the story. The National is a series of ten tests, but in 1947 the dogs were so evenly matched that it took twelve series or tests to find the winner. Here are examples that show just how simple these early tests were:

The fifth series: Land. Marked double, both birds 60 yards away with a spread of 40 yards between them.

The ninth series: Water. Combination marked and blind retrieve. A single marked bird shot 125 yards distant and across a channel. The blind was placed 70 yards across the channel on land. Without a winner declared after the ten required series, here is the test that separated the last four dogs that were carried all the way through to the twelfth series.

The twelfth series: Water. A single marked bird dropped into open land cover 80 yards distant and across water—a rather simple test by today's standards.

Forty years ago that work was worth a National. The average field-trial dog today could do those tests with one paw tied behind its back.

The dog that won that 1947 National was Bracken's Sweep, owned by Daniel E. Pomeroy and handled by Cotton Pershall. When the dog died in

1959, *Retriever Field Trial News* thought so much of his ability that they printed a front-page story praising the dog. "The record of 'Sweep,' " it said, "speaks for itself—he is another who justly deserves membership in the 'Retriever Hall of Fame' should there ever be one established."

Twenty years later, in 1968, the sixth series was a water blind that will show in comparison with the ninth series of 1947 the trend of things. Where the earlier blind was rather simple, 70 yards across a body of water and up on the land, this blind was a channel blind of 85 yards. The drawing reproduced from *Retriever Field Trial News* (July 1968) shows what we have been talking about.

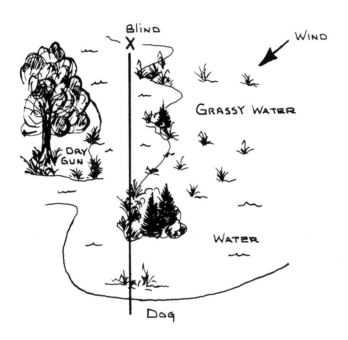

This blind retrieve takes the kind of control that the earlier dogs were not trained to attain. The line up through the channel, which is 40 yards wide, is very close to the right shore. The water is both running and swimming depth. Two *dry* shots were fired, to simulate shots by the hunter and indicate that a bird was winged and sailed on to where the blind was placed. This actually does not happen, and that is why it is called a "dry" shot. The dog sees no winged bird sailing and falling (there is no bird) to where the blind is planted. The whole point is, often in hunting, the hunter knows where the bird is and the dog does not—thus the name *blind retrieve*. But those two dry shots fired from the left side of the channel are a setup to try to fool the dog and have him "sucked in" toward that left bank. The clump of bushes in front of the dog is also a trap to make him go left. The handler must set his dog up, and the line to be taken is to "edge" the bush and take the line up the channel. "If you want supper don't set foot on land." In spite of the temptation of the points of land that jut out into the channel, twenty-seven dogs attempted this test, and only four failed.

We are seeing work here that would have astounded those early Scottish gamekeepers. We are seeing the retrievers being pushed to the limits of what an animal can do.

The great trainer Charles Morgan was one of the few who spanned the early period and continued into the time when the dogs were pushed to the outside edge of the realm of their learning. Talking about water blinds, he said, "The marks are just a set-up for the blind. Sometimes it looks as if the trials today were decided on water blinds, and often on one particular type of blind. It looks like it narrows down to what they call 'threading the needle.' I think it is unfortunate that these 'threading the needle' blinds so often decide a trial."

It is a shame that Charles Morgan did not live to see the amateur National in 1986. This is a good example of the "distance" phase of the testing. Whereas threading the needle in 1968 was done on an 85-yard blind, in 1986 it became 225 yards!

In 1968 the dogs were trained to swim the channel and not set a foot on land until directed to do so, as shown in the diagram from *Retriever Field Trial News* (December 1986).

Now the game has changed again. The line the dog must take (solid line in the diagram—ignore the broken line for the moment) is along the edge of a pond. Running the bank along the edge of the water would be the fastest way to the bird, but that is an absolute no-no! Earlier, the dogs were taught that when they enter water they must stay off the land. Now the dogs are asked to go land, water, edge the land, water, land, water, land, water, ignore the land, water, land, cross a road and make the retrieve. And the dog must do this after having seen a *poison* bird (a marked retrieve) thrown and shot. It's called a poison bird because the dog must not pick that bird up. He must ignore that shot bird and do the blind retrieve first. That's

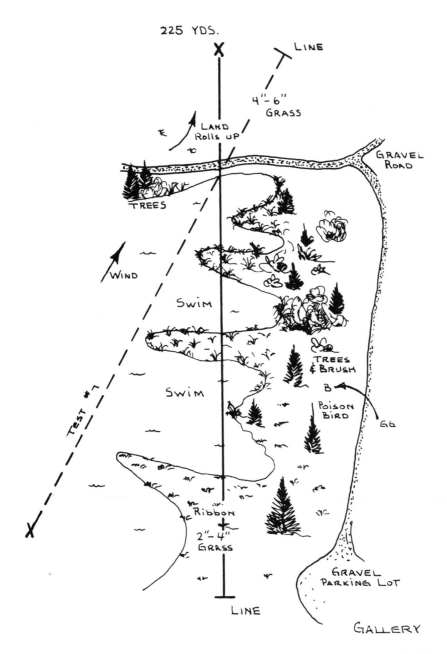

225 YDS.

X

LINE

4"-6"
GRASS

LAND
Rolls UP

GRAVEL
ROAD

TREES

WIND

Swim

TREES
& BRUSH

Swim

B

TEST

Poison
Bird

GG

Ribbon

2"-4"
GRASS

GRAVEL
PARKING LOT

X

LINE

GALLERY

a new kind of pressure being added to the judges' bag of tricks. While doing these blinds, the dog must not deviate from the course. Fifteen degrees off course is getting close to failing the test. Of the twenty-four still in the running that attempted this test, only nine failed.

Interestingly, the broken line in the diagram is the author's addition to make a point. If the test were reversed and the starting line was at the top of the drawing, in the field, the dogs would have handled the test as a channel blind. As some trainers say, "certain mind's-eye pictures bring up a specific response in the dog." The point is that the new bag of tricks does not eliminate the old fads. They are in addition, and all become part of the retriever's repertoire.

Where it goes from here and what will be required of these dogs in the future is anyone's guess.

The Training of the Retrievers

There seems to be no doubt that what evolved as the American field trial itself produced a dog of outstanding ability. The system of multiple marked retrieves developed a memory in the dog that is almost uncanny. When a handler takes a dog to line and the judges signal for the test to commence, the handler along with the dog has to mark the exact spot and remember it so that if the dog misses the mark the handler can, with whistle and hand signals, handle the dog to the spot. To do this the handler's brain has to work like a computer because the three birds will be shot or thrown in about fifteen seconds. Example, the fall of the first bird: on the hill—ninety-five yards away; on a line to the right-hand corner of the barn on the horizon; about five yards to the left of the bright green patch of weeds in the large stubble area—*remember green patch!* Second bird: seventy yards; at the edge of the woods; small evergreen; to the right of the black stump. Third bird is the dog's responsibility to mark and retrieve. But if, as in many of the hunting tests, the judge instructs the handler to have the birds picked up in a specific order, such as to retrieve the second bird down first, then handler and dog must use their "computer" on the third bird also.

If this is the mental process the handler must go through in order to remember the marked falls, what does the dog have to do? Doesn't it have to be much the same? Some say no. Some say the dog takes a general line to the bird, then uses its nose. That may be very true. Are there some days when there is no scent? Then what? Whatever the answer is, picking up the three marks is a remarkable feat.

The blind retrieve takes a different kind of skill. This is sheer obedience. Unlike the obedience work a dog does in the formal obedience ring, where the surroundings are controlled and never vary, today's field-trial or hunting retriever must obey at great distances (up to and over two hundred yards for the field-trial dog), and in all kinds of weather, terrain, water, or water and land, and with many different smells present. He must stop on whistle and take the appropriate cast from the handler's directional signal. These modern retrievers are now being asked to do "heavy" work as compared to our early retrievers and the British dog before them.

Tracing the training literature can give a good understanding of how the dogs developed.

The Training Literature

Although the very early writing on training won't answer our question about how our American dogs became so highly skilled, the tutelage makes interesting reading for those involved with retrievers. The sporting literature in England goes back to the fifteenth century, but it wasn't until the seventeenth century that anything appeared on waterfowl hunting and the training of dogs. Gervase Markham in 1655 wrote *Hungers Prevention: or, The Whole Art of Fowling by Water and Land.* The book has much charm, as a few quotations will demonstrate:

> Now for the manner of trayning or bringing up of this Water Dogge, it is to be understood that you cannot beginne too early with him, that is to say even when you first weane him, and teach him to lappe, for even then you shall beginne to teach him obedience, which is the maine thing that includeth all the lessons which he shall learne. Soone as it is able to lappe, you shall teach it to coutch and lye close, not daring to stirre or move from that posture.

> You must have no more teachers, no more feeders, cherishers, or correctors but one.

You must be very constant to the words of directions by which you teach, chusing such as are the most significant in your purpose, and fittest for the action and by no means alter that word which you first use.

You must understand the Doggie takes notice of the sound and not the English and therefore the least variation puts him into amazement, and is a language he understands not; as for example: if when you teach your Whelpe first to Couch, you use the word (Couch) if after you use the word (Downe) and not Couch, it will put the dogge into amazement and he will not know what to do.

There are thirteen pages of training hints in Markham's book. One piece of Markham's advice has been used in training books right into the twentieth century:

THE

GENTLEMAN'S

Recreation:

OF

FOWLING:

With a fhort Account of

Singing-Birds.

What Fowling is; with the Nature and Diverfity of all manner of Fowl.

FOWLING is ufed two Manner of Ways either by Enchantment, or Enticement; by winning or wooing the Fowl unto you by Pipe, Whiftle, or Call; or elfe by Engine, which unawares furprizeth them. Fowl are of divers Sorts, which alter in their Nature as their Feathers; but, by reafon of their multiplicity,

The Gentleman's Recreation, by Nicholas Cox, was the most important work of its day on fowling.

You shall then as you walk, drop something behind you which the Dogge may no see, and being gone a little way from it, send the Dogge back to fetch it, by saying, Back I have lost, or some such like, and if at first he stands amazed, urge him and sease not, by pointing your finger the way you would have him go, til he doe turn back and find the thing which you have dropt. Then drop it again and go twice as farre, and send the dog back to seeke and not leaving til you make him hunt & bring to you, then cherish and reward him.

Two books followed Markham, the first was *The Gentleman's Recreation* by Nicholas Cox, which was in four parts, "Hunting," "Hawking," "Fowling" and "Fishing." Printed in 1674, this book gives in the "Fowling" section a three-page abstract of the complete training section, which was absolutely stolen out of Markham's 1655 book. Then about 1740, but this

time spelled with an *e,* Nicholas Coxe's work was republished by the printer
Dixwell. (George Pugh, collector and scholar, after researching the matter
believes Cox and Coxe are the same person.) The fowling section of this
version of *The Gentleman's Recreation,* with a subtitle, "Dogs for Fowling,"
is almost a word-for-word copy of the 1674 *Gentleman's Recreation.* It also
contains the dog-training abstract from the original Markham book but in
a slightly expanded version. In spite of the fact that Cox plagiarized the
dog-training material from Markham's book, he was considered a very
knowledgeable person on all sorts of outdoor sports, and his books were
reprinted under different titles for a century and a half.

As there were no copyright laws in old England, it seems at first glance
that all the early, original writing on retriever training could be traced to the
work of Gervase Markham. But even this now seems doubtful. In his book
The History of Hunting (1936), Patrick Chambers makes Markham out as a
plagiarist, a "hack" journalist "with the sole idea of making money by writing. Entirely shameless in the way he plagiarized—not only the writings of
others, but his own as well—he was wont to publish the same book several
times over, under a different name." So we are not sure who originated
Markham's *Hungers Prevention.*

To give more of the early approach in retriever training, here are some
passages from the Cox abstract of Markham's book:

> You must teach him to fetch and carry any thing you throw out of your hands.
> And first try him with a glove, shaking it over his Head, and making him snap
> at it; and sometimes let him hold it in his mouth, and strive to pull it from
> him; and at last throw it a little way. . . .

> Now you may train him up for your Gun; making him stalk after you step by
> step, or else couch and lie close till you have shot. . . .

> The last use of the Water Dog [the old spelling of "dogge" has changed to
> "dog" somewhere between 1655 and 1674] is in moulting-time, when Wild-
> fowl cast their Feathers and are unable to fly, which is between Summer and
> Autumn. At this time bring your dog to their Coverts, and hunt them out
> into the stream; and there with your nets drive, and surprise them; for at this
> time sheep will not drive more easily.

All three books, in almost identical wording, go on to explain how to
take the birds in molt and fatten them up for the table.

After searching the New York library of the AKC, which has a most extensive dog collection, the British Kennel Club library in London, the excellent Chapin dog collection housed at William and Mary College's Swem library at Williamsburg, Virginia, and consulting George Pugh's private collection, I feel quite sure that there is no significant writing on the training of retrievers from the original writings of Markham in 1655 until the 1800s.

In 1829 Captain Thomas Brown, in his book *Anecdotes of Dogs,* describes a teaching method, based on instilling in the pup a desire to play the retrieve game, that was unique for his time.

> When puppies are five or six months old, they should be taught to fetch and carry. A method which has been successful is to get a rabbit's skin stuffed, and begin by tossing it about in a room. When the dog, which should have a small line to his collar, takes up the skin, bring him to you by a gentle pull with the skin in his mouth; encourage him three or four times, and then take the line off. When the dog begins to enjoy this sport, take a small line and run it through a pulley fixed to the ceiling, then tie the rabbit's skin to one end of the line and keep the other in your hand; after this fire a pistol and let the skin drop. The dog will soon become fond of the sport, and will thereafter readily bring every head of game and wild-fowl that is shot.

Many of our American outdoor sports have come down to us from England and been passed on to us in their literature. But subsequent British writing devoted to training retrievers, although rather late (1880s to early 1900s), is not very useful to the American sportsman, although most of the important English writers were reprinted in the United States by American publishers. Our most important outdoor writer, Frank Forester, edited an English book, *The Dog* by Dinks, Mayhew, and Hutchinson (Revised edition, 1878), adapting the verbiage for the American market. Many of these books tell more about dog management than *breaking,* which is the British word for training. Here are the important books:

John Johnson's book *The Dog; and How to Break Him,* published in 1851, is typical of the hunting literature of the time. It is mainly about pointing dogs with some reference to retrievers. Like most of the British writers, Johnson's material is not actually a training method but some practical hints. For example:

BIOGRAPHICAL SKETCHES

AND AUTHENTIC

ANECDOTES OF DOGS,

EXHIBITING

Remarkable Instances of the Instinct, Sagacity, and Social Disposition of
this Faithful Animal: Illustrated by Representations of the most
Striking Varieties, and by correct Portraits of

CELEBRATED OR REMARKABLE DOGS,

FROM

Drawings chiefly Original.

ALSO,

A HISTORICAL INTRODUCTION;

AND

A COPIOUS APPENDIX

ON THE BREEDING, FEEDING, TRAINING, DISEASES, AND
MEDICAL TREATMENT OF DOGS;

TOGETHER WITH A

TREATISE ON THE GAME LAWS OF GREAT BRITAIN.

BY CAPTAIN THOMAS BROWN,

F.R.S.E., F.L.S., M.R.P.S.E., M.W.S., &c.

Author of " Illustrations of the Conchology of Great Britain and Ireland," and of
" General Ornithology," &c.

EDINBURGH:

PUBLISHED BY

OLIVER & BOYD, TWEEDDALE-COURT;

AND

SIMPKIN & MARSHALL, LONDON.

1829.

Title page of Captain Thomas Brown's important book, 1829.

Sometimes it will happen, though not often, that a young dog will bite his game too hard; and this is an unfortunate circumstance. If a rabbit skin be stuffed with hard straw, with thorns intermixed, and used for him to fetch and carry, in the first instance, it will not often happen that he will bite his game; but should he acquire that habit, a dead bird—a pigeon, for instance—may be stuck through with sharp wire, which will prick his mouth when he attempts to squeeze too much, and may eventually cure him of a practice which will be likely to increase with age.

Today that advice is still good.

Many of the writers like Johnson tell the reader what to expect in the dog but not how to accomplish it. For example, Johnson wrote: "There are three things necessary in the retriever's education:—never to leave the heel unless ordered to do so; to remain stationary to drop on the firing of the gun; and to fetch to his master the dead or wounded game." And that is it.

Two books came out about the same time in the early 1880s, *Dog Breaking* by General W. N. Hutchinson and *Breaking and Training Dogs* containing sections by "Pathfinder" (pseudonym for H. C. Deare) and Hugh Dalziel. Hutchinson is possibly the best-known dog writer of his day and the most quoted. Dalziel is best known for his books on dogs and their care. Pathfinder, in the book with Dalziel, gives one of the few step-by-step training procedures in the British literature. Pathfinder's section in *Breaking and Training Dogs* is by far the best English work on training the retrievers. Whereas Hutchinson devotes eighteen pages to "Lessons in Fetching" (for all hunting dogs), fewer than ten pages are on what he calls "Regular Land Retrievers." Much of his writing consists of narrative stories about dogs or situations he remembers. It seems that he set the pattern for this kind of narrative writing, storytelling about training, and most dog writers that followed him used this same technique.

Pathfinder, at the beginning of his sixty pages on retriever training, spells out exactly what he will cover: "When I have explained the process of fetch and carry, I will go on to describe how to teach him, secondly, to 'drop and stay'; thirdly, to 'turn and come to whistle or name'; fourthly, 'come in and keep to heel'; fifthly, 'water work'; and last 'trailing and hunting.' These are the necessary groundwork and foundation stones. . . ." But Pathfinder's work, by far the best of this period, was overshadowed by Hutchinson's narrative stories!

About the turn of the century there were two British books devoted solely to retrievers; neither of them carries a date of publication, but on reading it's easy to date them by content. *Retrievers and How to Break Them*, by Sir Henry Smith, published by William Blackwood and Sons, must date from about 1898. (In the text he dates an anecdote as happening in the shooting season of 1896; thus dating the publishing at about 1898 seems correct.) In true English style he, too, instructs by example, using the Hutchinson narrative method of explaining his points. The author tells stories of dogs and keepers, the accomplishments and mistakes of both, and then gives his own explanatory suggestions. This book makes charming reading, with a lot of scattered, useful information that is more background material than training manual.

The Scientific Education of Dogs for the Gun by H. H., published by Sampson Low, Marston & Company of London, is one of the best-written of the British books. Again the date of publication is not given, but in my copy of the third edition there is a foreword dated 1910. I can only make a guess that the author, H. H., might be The Honorable A. Holland-Hibbert, who later became Lord Knutsford and the founder of the English Labrador club. This book seems to have a little more of the step-by-step approach to training, but oh, how the British sportsman loves his story telling. Example?

H. H. writes:

> When an undergraduate at Oxford, I had a very clever smooth-coated retriever, and I had broken her to "back fetch." [Note that the Markham training method of year 1655, dropping an object for the dog to run back and find, is still being used. H. H. describes it as when you drop a tobacco pouch or handkerchief on the ground and tell the dog to leave it. Then walk on a good distance and send the dog back for the dropped item. The author says he could send the dog as far as a mile. It is a retrieving technique all of the early trainers used.] One day I was out walking with a friend, and we had got to the top of Headington Hill, about two miles from Oxford. I put my hand in my pocket for my pipe, a short meerschaum in a case, and found I had left it behind, and remembered putting it on the table of my lodging just before I started. "I wonder whether Duchess will fetch it," I asked my friend; "lend me your pipe, and I'll try it." I showed her the pipe in the case, and said, "Go back, fetch mine, there's a good girl." She looked at me for a moment, and

According to the earliest writings on the subject, training started with the dropping of an object for the dog to go back and fetch.

then away she went best pace. We sat down on a stile and waited, and in about twenty minutes she appeared with the pipe all right. I heard afterwards from a man who occupied the room over mine, that he was disturbed in his reading by the violent barking of a dog at the street door. He looked out the window and saw Duchess tearing at it tooth and nail, and barking enough to raise the dead. He went down and opened the door; she rushed past him upstairs, and, before he got half way up, repassed him with a growl with my pipe in her mouth. I always thought she must have seen me lay it down, but anyhow it was a good feat.

The tobacco pouch becomes a training tool to teach the dog to fetch by sight and then by nose. Stewart Smith, in his book *Retrievers and How to Break Them for Sport and Field Trials,* published by The Field Press Ltd., London, no date but apparently from the first decade of the twentieth century, uses the pouch to teach the dog to be at ease in the water:

> There are plenty of shootings where dogs never require to wet their feet from one year's end to another; but the title of this book is *Retrievers and How to Break Them for Sport and Field Trials,* and as more than one field trial (particularly at Norwich) has been won by good work in the water—and at future meetings this test will no doubt become an imperative one—I lay great stress on this part of the retriever's education. In order to teach him, when young, to take to water readily, there is nothing to surpass the good old way of walking yourself through a stream or brook, very narrow and very shallow to begin with. Where you go the dog will surely follow; if not a very little coaxing will do so. You can take advantage at this stage, give him a few lessons in bringing your pouch from the other side of the stream. You may do this in two ways, either throw the thing over and then send him for it, or leave it, walk over the stream, and then send him to back fetch.

Major W. G. Eley's book *Retrievers and Retrieving,* published in London in 1905 by Longmans, Green, and Company, adds little that is new to the "art" of breaking a retriever. About young dogs he writes, "As a general rule, the age at which the instructor can begin to teach Retrievers their business is from three months to eight months old—a fairly elastic period, which is liable to alteration. Had I only one age to select from, I should choose a forward puppy of about six months." He amplifies on the work a young dog should do, which is "light" and not much of it.

About a young pup he says, "Think twice before continuing your lessons until you are sure the puppy will learn with pleasure. You would not try to cram learning into a baby's brain without expecting to do harm, and a puppy comes under the same category." An interesting and understandable comment for that time but one proved to be quite wrong much later in the century.

A popular book, Frank Townsend Barton's *The Retriever,* published in London, by Everett and Company, devotes only seven pages to breaking but for its day is very good on care of the retrievers. As with so many English books, there is no date of publication. From its contents (he gives a big play to the Flat-Coated Retriever) it would seem that the book was published in the last part of the nineteenth century or very early twentieth.

A guess would be that 80 percent of the contents of these English books is taken up with narrative stories of experiences in the field, following the style of the popular and successful writer Hutchinson. One of the first books devoted only to retrievers was *Observations on Breaking Retrievers* by F. R. Bevan, published in the 1880s (its fourth edition appeared in 1891). Like all the others, in their charming but rambling Hutchinsonian way, Bevan's book covers much the same material, obedience work. All the books tell you to spare the rod and gain confidence. They all introduce the dog to the gun, the game, and the field. They tell of dogs and gamekeepers that did not work out and glowing stories of those that did. In spite of the word *scientific* being in the title of one of the books, none of them approaches the training problems in a scientific manner, but they are all fun reading. The British books all lacked the same thing: no one produced a popular step-by-step training manual for the beginner, the new hunter, except Pathfinder—he produced it, but unfortunately somehow its path got lost.

If the British training literature had to be expressed in one sentence, it could be: The dog is given excellent obedience training, an introduction to its field job, and then allowed to develop on its own.

It seems quite evident that the men who wrote the books were not the men who were doing the serious training of the dogs. The gamekeepers and gillies were the handlers of the dogs, but they could hardly write their names, let alone a book.

Dog-Training Books on the American Scene

America for over a hundred years has produced some excellent step-by-step manuals on the training of the pointing dogs. *Practical Dog Training* by S. T. Hammond, published in New York in 1884, was well known. For retriever training, we relied on the British writers. The English books, as we have seen, left a lot to be desired. Much of their work was also published in America. For example, *Dog Training,* edited by "Ashmont" (Dr. J. Frank Perry's pseudonym), is an Americanized version of W. C. Percy's book. It was published in Boston in 1886. It adds little or nothing of value to the literature. During the period of the 1890s and the turn of the century, when these British books were being produced and republished in the United States, there were so few working retrievers in America that a book on their training would hardly have had a big enough audience to justify the publishing expense.

History often plays tricks. Out of the "clear blue sky" in 1895 a gem of a book called *Fetch and Carry* was written by B. Waters and published in New York by Forest and Stream Publishing Company. There were not that many retrievers around or hunters who used them, so it's hard to figure why this book was written and published.

Fetch and Carry is the most comprehensive book to come along and is much ahead of its time. In the main section of the book, Waters offers two methods of training the dog in the retrieving job, the natural system and the force system, with a detailed and clear step-by-step explanation. Although he was the first to mention these two methods as they applied to the working retriever, he does it as well or better than many of the writers that have come after him. The two systems, natural and force, will be discussed in Chapter 7.

The book covers every phase of the training. In the chapter "Seeking Dead and Wounded Birds," he even manages to cover, in the section on trailing, the rudiments of teaching the dog to follow hand signals, the beginning of handling, which was something in the dog's training that was not done until forty years later.

The book is about more than training the dog. Waters gives sensible advice to the amateur trainer on qualities to cultivate, control of his temper, tone of voice, necessity of self-discipline, theory of dog intelligence, and much more. It is a well-organized book.

He has chapters on the Irish Water Spaniel and the Chesapeake Bay Retriever and a section on English retrievers, which was written by Captain C. E. McMurdo of Charlottesville, Virginia. We get no hint from the book about who McMurdo was or, for that matter, who B. Waters was. It took quite a search to find that his first name was Bernard and that he at times wrote under the pen name of "Kingrail," but we have no idea where he was from. He comes across in his writing as a very intelligent and well-educated man. He sets out in his writing to produce a unique book: referring to retrievers in his preface, he states, "no author, so far as I know, has given the subject special consideration and amplification." He did!

This book is a first. It just seems so out of place in the literature. If Waters had been British and the book had come at the end of the long line of writers on the subject of training retrievers, it would have seemed natural. For him to have been the first American writer on this subject and to produce a book with such advanced ideas, even ahead of today's English authors, proves him to be a man of vision and talent. If this book had a chapter on teaching handling of the retrievers, as it is done now, it could be a best-seller today. The book is a treasure and can be found in the used-book shops.

Just where his material for the natural and force-training methods came from is not known. They must have been his original ideas, but he does not present them as a new system. He presents them in a matter-of-fact way and explains them in depth. Just how popular the B. Waters book was is hard to say. There seems to be very little other information or writing on the retrievers from the time Waters wrote the book in 1894 until the late 1920s. The Scottish gamekeepers who were doing the dog training in America had no need for a book since they brought their own know-how with them from Scotland.

After Waters's book, for the next fifty years, no training book of any real value was produced. There was little need for one, because most of the dogs that showed up in America were trained by the professionals. The picture changed during the 1930s, when the retrievers became a major factor on the American hunting scene.

Now Mr. Joe Average Hunter was in the act. Dave D. Elliot, the "inventor of handling" of the retrievers and one of the most important trainers on the scene, published *Training Gun Dogs to Retrieve* with Henry Holt in 1952. He was a better dog trainer and handler than a writer. Socially prominent early Labrador owner Kathleen B. Starr and gun dog editor for *Field and Stream* magazine Joe Stetson "helped" Dave produce the book. It is very charming and tells much about the early field-trial days in America, but his book was not a big success because it tried to be two things at once: a narrative story and a training book when what was needed at that time, by the new hunter using retrievers, was a complete training manual.

Such a book did come on the scene just a few years before Elliot produced his book, and it was an immediate success. *Training Your Retriever* by James Lamb Free, published by Coward McCann, was announced with a fine review in the May 1949 issue of *Retriever Field Trial News*.

The reviewer says in part:

> Here is a book packed full of information. To quote the publishers, "A new kind of book—by an impatient man—for impatient men—for every duck hunter and gunner of upland game who yearns to own his own retriever—who wants to know how to go about finding and training his own dog quickly and easily—without spending half his life at it."
>
> It is all of this with a lot to spare. The publisher gave permission to quote in a periodical or radio review up to 750 words. Your editor has read this 227 pages three times and looked at the 125 illustrations at least a dozen times. We have tried to figure some way to give proper description and proper credit in 750 words. It just can't be done.

Free started his retriever training in 1938 and became heavily involved with field trials. As an amateur writing for the amateur, he had two things going for him: he was a good trainer and a good writer. He learned the business of training from the famous Hogan family, Martin the father, daughter Mary, and sons Frank and Jim. The Waters book was the first step in the American literature, and it left the British system far behind. The Free book was an easy step-by-step approach, and it established the American training method.

Although the 1949 Free book became the "bible," a book that was to outsell it was published in 1963. My own book *Water Dog* had a difficult start in the marketplace, but the little guy, the hunter, had such success with it that by word of mouth it soon vastly outsold the Free book. The problem was that the old-line trainers and field trialers could not imagine starting a puppy when it was only seven weeks old, and they went out of their way to demonstrate their displeasure with the new book. They believed as Free did that you didn't start a pup's training until it was about a year old. This new, early-training method, dubbed *Revolutionary, Rapid Training Method* by E. P. Dutton, the publishers, was the result of the findings of the animal behaviorists at the Hamilton Station, Bar Harbor, Maine, who did a major study on learning in the dog, in conjunction with the Guide Dogs for the Blind, Inc. This book was not written for the field trialer or the professional trainer. It was for the little guy who wanted to have a puppy in his home as a member of the family, a dog that was the children's pet and the master's hunting companion. After a stormy beginning, the book and the early-training method have been accepted. The scientific data behind the book's training program could not be refuted, and new books written today include that early-training information. As a spokesman for the publisher said, "You don't make over thirty big printings of a book if it doesn't work for the public." My aim was to translate the "scientificese" into simple "dogese" that the hunter could understand. Five thousand pictures were taken for the book, and all the material is presented to the reader three ways: first in text; then the same material in running sequence pictures that show what the text is about; then in the captions and caption blocks as a short repeat of the text. After a quarter of a million copies were sold, the book was revised to include upland work and called *Game Dog*. Now both books take the hunter from the starting point, a seven-week-old pup, to the finished dog.

Many books have been written on the training of the retrievers since Free's book and mine, but they say nothing that is new. A two-hour videotape also shows the step-by-step training procedures of *Game Dog*.

For the average hunter, the training procedures are now well established, and these books will do the job. But for the licensed field trialer whose dog is a precision machine, there are several good books to produce these results. *Training Retrievers to Handle* by D. L. and Ann Walters is an important book. Published by the authors in 1979, the book deals only with the handling of the dog. It is a very natural method of building from simple exercises to complex patterns, which are shown in diagrams and explained in the text. Any handler who puts himself and his dog through this program will have astonishing results.

D. L. and Ann Walters produced another book that gives a lot of good information for the field trialer and the hunter. The book is based on a series of taped interviews called *Charles Morgan on Retrievers*. There is a lot of information in the book that will be found nowhere else. It starts with the pup and takes you through every step of the way to the finished dog, including problems. Morgan's recollections of the early days make for fun reading. The two books produced by the Walterses are outstanding parts of the retriever literature.

Two other books deserve a mention. *Retriever Training Tests* by James B. Spencer (Arco, 1983) shows you how to set up training tests to teach yourself and the dog all the pitfalls there are out in the field. Another good general reading book, beautifully produced, and chock-full of good training advice, is Tom Quinn's *The Working Retrievers,* published in 1983 by E. P. Dutton.

Starting with the Markham book in 1655 and now some 330 years later, these few books discussed are the more important books in the training literature in the retriever world.

6

Looking Out for Our American Retrievers

We have gone back in time to give you a perspective on the retriever world. In this chapter, the main focus will be on the American hunter. At present, there are serious problems for both the hunter and his retriever.

Much of the American sporting world, as we have seen, had its origins in Great Britain. That is especially true in the dog world. Our own American Kennel Club was patterned after the English Kennel Club. Retriever history demonstrates that what developed in Britain and was perpetuated by their strong sense of tradition has been a hindrance to the development of their retrievers for hunting. With our American club patterned after the British club in many ways, the same thing has happened over here.

The hunting population in Britain is very small. Their field trialers can supply enough puppies for the sportsman. So the hunters use field-trial stock and the field-trial training methods that have come down to them from their grandfathers—with little or no change.

The discussion is not whether this is right or wrong. We are not trying to influence or change what the British think about their dog or their sport.

However, we must make sure that what has happened across the ocean does not happen here. Except for a relatively few field Labradors in Great Britain, the breed is no longer a hunting dog. Unfortunately, generations of Labradors in England do not get the opportunity to hunt and the skill has been lost. This is something Americans should consider when buying pups with "English" blood.

Both the American and the British kennel clubs have allowed the mainstream of the breeding of their retrievers to lose the purpose for which they were originally developed. Unfortunately, the American club, following the English lead, is so tradition-bound that it neither will nor can act as the protector of our dogs' hunting skills. Yet national kennel clubs on the European continent do exert that authority. When they have a serious problem, such as a hunting dog no longer able to hunt, they step in to force the member breed club "to go back to the drawing board" and make breeding changes.

It takes centuries of concentrated effort to make a hunting dog and fewer than forty years to undo the work. Dogs don't get into that kind of a fix themselves, and neither the hunter nor the field trialer can be held responsible. The blame belongs to the show ring and the resultant market.

When the problem of protecting a hunting breed's working future was presented to the American Kennel Club, it took the position that it was a club of clubs and had no right to tell a member club what to do. In a speech to the Dog Writers' Association of America in 1985, I asked how the AKC could stand by and watch a working dog "go down the drain," and what the AKC's founding fathers would say if they could return and see that so many hunting dogs that have become popular in the show ring can no longer hunt. The only answer was that the AKC was a club of clubs with no right to interfere.

Should the AKC constitution be changed to give it policing powers to protect the dogs? But the popularity of a dog leads to a bigger pet market, which in turn results in increased dog registrations. As a governing body, the AKC will not bite the hand that feeds it.

Most breed clubs are run by show people. They write the physical standard for the dog, which unfortunately over a period of time tends to become a standard of fads having little or no functional purpose. As one irate Husky owner said, "No wonder our dogs can't work anymore. Not one member of the standards committee ever saw a dog-sled team work."

Although the Golden Retriever Club of America is basically a show

The Golden is so popular that its hunting future is in jeopardy. *(Becky Mills Photo)*

club, it truly and actively is trying to keep the work in the breed, but it is faced with a losing situation. The Golden is so handsome and has such a fine disposition that the general dog public has taken this breed to its heart. The Golden, in a very few years, has become the fourth most popular breed in America. The problem: As a hunting dog, from hunting stock, it is a good worker in this field, but in this writer's opinion, it's not as strong a hunter as either the Lab or the Chessie, because the show people have taken it over. This means that there are not enough hunters championing the breed to protect it from the effects of the increased breeding for the show ring and pet market. The expanding numbers, show versus hunting, are against this dog. As a worker, its future, twenty or forty years down the road, is bleak.

The handwriting is on the wall, but you will see as you read on that we now know how to prevent a breed from slipping onto the "no longer hunter" list. Unfortunately, a major segment of the Golden Retriever people are not doing much about it.

The Labrador Retriever Club

The Labrador story is different. At its inception in 1931, the Labrador Retriever Club was strongly field-oriented. It ran the first retriever trial, as we have said, in December 1931. It ran field trials again in 1932 and 1933. It was not until 1933 that it held its first breed show.

One fact shows how field-oriented the Labrador Retriever Club was in its first show: there were thirty-three dogs entered and they were the same dogs, with same owners, that had been in the first field trial. The winners at the trial were also the winners at the show. The dogs entered were working dogs. Mrs. Marshall Field, whose dog had won the first trial in 1931, was the show judge in this first event. The dogs she was judging for conformation were hunting dogs.

That show was held in the basement garage of the Marshall Fields' Fifth Avenue town house. Jim Cowie recalled that it was not a very happy occasion. First of all, he claimed that the lighting was poor in the basement and he could not see how "anyone could make a good judgment about black dogs in a coal bin." But Jim said that that was not the main reason for the occasion's being unhappy. He recalled that it was a Sunday in May (actually the nineteenth) and that all the gamekeepers had to bring their owners' dogs into New York City from as far away as Tuxedo, New York, and the eastern end of Long Island, on their day off, to run their dogs in a circle like sissies.

From that first show for Labradors in 1933, interest has grown so that there are now almost a thousand shows a year. As the popularity of a dog explodes, as in the case of the Golden and the Lab, the emphasis in the show ring goes from work to pet-market sales. The people who gain the position of being responsible to the breed for its development are far too often not hunters and can do little more than train a dog to stand and heel in a show ring. With the hunting breeds, they give lip service to the work, but most don't hunt or know how to train a working dog.

*   *   *

In the early days of the Labrador Retriever Club, there was no question that field trials were the main purpose of the club's activities. The Labrador club members were actually the nucleus of the retriever field activities in America. The club was mainly a wealthy sporting group. But because it was the breed club representative to the AKC, it also had to be responsible for the show activities and the writing of the standard.

Since field trials were the driving interest of the club's officers and members, the show activities, considered a necessary but secondary function, were delegated to one of the club's board of directors, James Warwick, who with his wife, Helen, was very much interested in the show end of the dog game. The show function of the club's activities was happily turned over to them. Helen Warwick was in a powerful position. For twenty years she wrote on retriever matters for the *AKC Gazette*. They were a very classy couple and spent much of their time in England. The club soon came to function this way: If your local club wanted judges for its show, it might be a good idea to contact the Labrador Retriever Club's show director, Jim Warwick, to get his opinion. Helen and Jim selected the judges for your club. If it was an important specialty, they might even take the assignment themselves. Or if it tickled your club's fancy to import a British judge, whom you could entertain while here, it might be arranged by the Warwicks. With the right judges, your show might be written up in the *AKC Gazette*. And if you really wanted your dogs to make their mark in the ring, it might be possible to get some English bloodline into your stock. Helen knew every British breeder and could get the exact dog you needed when she was next in England. If you enjoyed being a judge, wanted more assignments, and a good write-up for the show world to read, it might be to your advantage to pay attention to the dogs with that English "look." The Warwicks were invited to judge on both sides of the Atlantic. They controlled the game.

When Mrs. Warwick was interviewed by me, she was asked if it was important whether a British judge who comes to America should know how the American dog is used in the field. "No," she answered. "In the show ring, they divorce it completely from work; it is just for looks and nothing else. They don't even ask, 'Can a dog pick up a dummy?' " For Mrs. Warwick to suggest and then arrange for English judges for our show ring might have been pleasant socially for those involved, but it was a disservice to our dogs. The British judges often were also breeders. They didn't hunt their dogs in

The show ring has done harm to all the hunting breeds, not just retrievers. *(Author Photo)*

their country; their dogs were not used by the sportsman in England; the judges never even saw the hunting in America. Yet it was they who became the last word and advised our people on how to breed our dogs.

While this Anglophile show activity was happening on the show side of the Labrador Retriever Club, the field side took a directly opposite tack. It had no interest in shows and paid no attention to what was happening at them. After the first fifteen or so years of the Lab's coming into America, there was enough good working stock to start breeding the kind of dog who could best do the American work. This was the time, through the 1950s, 1960s, and 1970s, when the dog work was changing and progressing by leaps and bounds, leaving the British working retriever far behind. The English show-stock dog was no longer a hunter. It was useless for the American working and trialing scene, not just because of its lack of hunting skill but because of the fads that had gone into its physical makeup. Jokingly, it had been often said that a good, hard day's work on our Eastern Shore would kill one of the stocky, stubby, short-necked show dogs with what the

English call substance or "bone." With the head so blocky and muzzle and neck so short, it could be a battle royal between such a dog and a wounded goose—and most American hunters would put their money on the goose.

The members of the Labrador Retriever Club and all other field people rejected this dog Helen Warwick was touting in her column and in the corridors of the show ring. The English dogs flooded into America, however, and I am not sure the breed will ever recover.

The Labrador Retriever Club had both hands, field and show, working at the same time—in opposite directions.

The English field dog didn't do so well either in America. One wealthy member of the club, at great expense, bought one of the top, proven English field champions and brought him to America to "clean up" on the field-trial circuit. Not only did he fail to make it through the first trial, but his name seems to have been forgotten. Another member tried the same thing with the same result.

The show and field people have never seen eye to eye and have gone their own separate ways in spite of the Labrador club's written standard. They do not think much of each other's dogs; the show people refer to the working retriever as a "Whippet," and the field trialers refer to the show dog as a "pig." When asked about the standard, one field trialer said, "If I could find a black monkey who could mark down birds, take a line, run a snappy blind and guarantee me a win, I'd register him and run him!"

What the Hunter Knew

In the late 1930s and early 1940s, hunters started using Labradors, and then a little later Goldens, in the duck blind. The average hunter didn't know very much about how to train or work with a hunting retriever. The dogs worked mostly by their own natural instinct.

When B. Waters wrote his book *Fetch and Carry* in 1895, he had this to say about the American sportsman and his retriever:

A slovenly and disobedient retriever will mar the best of sport. However willing a dog may be to obey and perform, if he does not know methods and commands, he can add little to the pleasure or success of a shooter. The hunter is commonly satisfied with too low a standard of retrieving. His own standard of sport is not any too high. He is eager to capture regardless of method, and his eagerness many times is the source of unseemly scrambles between himself and the dog to get possession of the bird.

Waters did not have too high a regard for his colleagues. But there was little training information available for the average hunter.

After the Great Depression, the sport of field trialing began a constant, steady growth. At that time, the game was still dominated by the wealthy field trialers who had the dogs professionally trained; it was their social game and they kept it hard to crack. At that time, the little fellow had practically no chance of winning against the professionals. The hunter had a hard time even getting into the sport in certain snobbish eastern areas. The clubs and people to the west were more democratic. The hunters soon became involved, on the fringes of the game, because it was the only way they could learn how to train and handle a dog. Many became infatuated with field trials and became active members of a club. But it was difficult. Field trialing on the licensed circuit was expensive, so most of the hunters, the little guys,

Putting on a field event takes a lot of work by a lot of people. *(Author Photo)*

played the game on the local-sanction and fun-trial level. This offered little or no reward for them or recognition for their dogs.

Why did they do it? For some, it was the fun of playing with one's dog and getting it trained during the nonhunting season. For others, it was a way of trying to break into that eastern social set. Some managed all right on Saturday afternoon at the trial but not for cocktails and dinner Saturday night.

Putting on a licensed field trial is a big job needing lots of people. The clubs needed workers, and it was the hunter in many cases who became the workhorse during the event. It was a thankless organizational job: arranging for and handling birds, bird throwers, lunches for judges, hot drinks or cold drinks, shotgun shells, bag boys, marshals, parking committee, hostess committee—the list goes on. The contestants rolled in Thursday night and rolled out Sunday night, and the workers worked Monday to get the grounds back in perfect condition. It was like a beehive: there were performers (the queens) and drones.

In the early 1960s, a movement was started by the workers, who were basically hunters, to get something going that they could relate to. An informal event was proposed. It would carry no championship points and was to be called the Amateur Handler Stake. To be eligible a dog had to be owned by an amateur, handled by an amateur, and never have been trained by a professional.

The idea started with the Westchester Retriever Club in Westchester County, New York, and was to be a regional event involving the clubs in the northeastern part of the country. It would rotate each year to another club in the region. The purpose was to find the best hunting dog in the region, and the winner would receive a gold pin of the club that sponsored the event.

The Amateur Handler Stake, in some small way, was to repay the hunter and little guy and gal who were doing all the club's work. It was to give them and their dogs a purpose in the sport and to keep them interested in their club. The licensed trials could not have been put on without the workers. Yet when this concept of a hunters' stake reached the ears of the "ruling class" on Long Island, it was squashed, but hard. The only person from that wealthy, social set who came to the defense of a stake for the hunter was Louise Belmont, wife of August Belmont. Belmont was chairman of the board of directors of the AKC and was consulted and asked for advice before the organization for the Amateur Handler Stake was started. He agreed with the idea, gave it his blessing, but changed his mind after the stake was announced. Without him behind the movement, it was doomed.

This whole concept was to try to make a place for the hunter in the formal game of field trials. It failed.

The hunters, and there were hundreds of thousands of them with retrievers, were in a ridiculous situation. The AKC had taken their dog and made a formal place for it in the show world and in the field-trial game and left them out in the cold. The hunter had no organization and therefore no input into the future of his dog. He didn't even know where to get hunting stock pups when he needed them. The hunter didn't know who hunted in the next county, let alone what dogs they had or if they were any good.

The dogs that were available to the hunter, advertised in every Sunday newspaper, were show stock that, thanks to Warwick's reign, were ruined for hunting. The average hunter would not know how to get a pup from the field trialer, even if he could afford the high price, and the field-trial game could not supply the number of dogs needed by the millions of hunters.

The Hunter's Dilemma and the First Solution

The number of hunters who became involved, even as working bees, in field trials was only a small fraction of the hunters in the country. But they had well-trained dogs, and they were noticed wherever they hunted. For the first time, the average hunter was seeing a controlled dog that was trained to work.

Then the function of field trials changed. In the 1970s and 1980s, to find the four best dogs in the stake, field trials no longer simulated a day in the hunting field, but evolved into a game unto themselves. The average hunter was not interested. Nor was the show ring any place for him. The hunters and the ladies in the show game did not mix.

As the old-time field trialers disappeared from the game, a change initiated by the "working base" slowly took place.

At first, it started out as an informal gun dog stake, a modified field trial, a fun event with tests that the hunter and his dog could relate to and could accomplish. Where and when it started is a bit controversial—it just started to appear and grew.

This new field event had no formal rules. It was whatever the club and judges wanted it to be. It was educational for the hunter and his dog, fun, informal, and sometimes hilarious, as was the case of one gun dog trial I judged in the early 1960s. My co-judge was Ed Zern, the writer of the humorous "Exit Laughing" column on the last page of *Field and Stream* magazine. Ed had a lot of new ideas for testing the hunter and his dog under simulated hunting conditions. First we asked the field-trial committee to build a blind for the hunter and the dog to sit in, just like the real thing. After a lot of head scratching, the committee put such a contraption to-gether and covered it, at Ed's insistence, with reeds and branches. Then he ordered half a dozen sandwiches to be delivered to the blind. His idea was that all hunters have the same problem when they stop shooting for early morning breakfast in the blind. Simulating the problem, Ed had the hunter set a sandwich down on the bench "as the birds were flying in . . . and he reaches for his gun." That's when bird boys threw birds and the hunter shot them. At that point the dog was to be sent for the bird. Ed contended that the dog should be scored not only on the retrieving job, but be *marked down according to the amount of sandwich the dog downed.* Some dogs managed to get a whole sandwich, gobbling it down all the way to the downed bird.

Things didn't go so well in the second series either. We used the same blind; the handler was to stand up and shoot a blank as the bird was thrown fifty yards away—that was fine. But when Ed called for a tub of water, inside the blind, for the handler to stand in, the contestants balked—that was not fine. Ed casually explained that he *always* hunted ducks with wet feet. We got our way—that was fine. When Ed and I insisted that the committee produce a flower-sprinkling can so the marshal could pour water over the handler's head as he waited in the blind with his dog, Ed explaining that "We always hunted in the rain," that was *not* fine. The field-trial committee threatened to banish both judges from the grounds—they did—and that was fine. Ed and I went to a bar and contemplated the good old days when hunters were the backbone of the country and made it strong and bluebird weather was for those sissy golf players.

Gun-dog stakes became more and more popular each year. Some clubs were formed for the sole purpose of running three or four events for the

Events for the hunting dog are designed to simulate real hunting conditions. *(A. H. Rowan, Jr., Photo)*

hunter. These tests were held off-season, and the entries became quite big. Some of the licensed field-trial clubs started to hold similar events as money-makers. But the AKC did not participate in this new game, which was a by-product of their licensed game.

Clubs got together and formed associations. One of the big ones was Pendelmarva: Pennsylvania, Delaware, Maryland, and Virginia. The rules and the judging were a catch-as-catch-can affair. They tried to find the best dogs and give them placements, one to four, in different categories: puppies, gun dogs, and super gun dogs.

The boys and gals up in Vermont were playing the game and had a fine set of rules for their event, which they called the Classic. In Louisiana, the biggest duck-hunting state in the nation, a series of hunting dog clubs followed along with their own Pendelmarva concept, but it was all in-state. The outdoor magazines were telling the hunter what a trained retriever should be able to do. Now the hunter wanted his dog to be trained for this work, and this could be the place to do it.

Most of this gun-dog activity was taking place within the AKC-licensed clubs, but as an activity only of the clubs rather than the national organization. In the early 1980s, after many hundred of these events had been run, over many years, the AKC director of field trials wrote, "We are not entirely familiar with what you refer to as 'gun dog trials,' nor do we have any knowledge of how widespread this particular activity might be within the United States."

GUN DOG MAGAZINE GETS INTO THE ACT

In the early 1980s, two things happened together. While the gun-dog stake was spreading around the country, a new magazine, *Gun Dog,* hit the market. As the retriever columnist for the new magazine, I obviously would report on this phenomenon. I was invited by John and Debbie Morgan, both top-flight licensed AKC field trialers, to come to Virginia to see the AKC's licensed James River Club gun-dog stake. It was run as a club activity, not with AKC sanction.

The event proved to be a tremendous success. Everyone had a fun time, and handlers and dogs alike learned a lot. The hunter participation was so big that, that evening after the event (although many had gone home), 250 hot dogs were consumed at the club cookout.

That gun-dog stake was reported in the May/June 1982 issue of *Gun Dog.* Astonishingly, the response was almost overwhelming; hunters from all over the country were just as enthusiastic as they were in Virginia and wanted more information. The requests didn't come only from individuals, but from clubs, and they asked for rules or guidelines for such an event.

Publisher Dave Meisner, who at that point owned the magazine, was ecstatic over the response. We set out to give the readers what they wanted. Dave Maynard, a hunter and member of the Westchester Retriever Club, and I sat down and drafted a set of rules or guidelines that we thought would work. After testing the rules with a few hunters and their dogs, we turned the rules over to the Westchester club in June 1982, and they ran an event using them. Harvey and Edna Gardenier, experienced hunters, dog people, and judges, set up tests that eliminated the artificial aspects of field trials and simulated hunting situations.

Ned Spears recalls that when his dog Penny Rose finished a blind retrieve, the gallery of hunters applauded. This was also the first time since the early 1940s that a retriever was required to do upland hunting.

The event went off with enthusiasm, like clockwork, and was reported in the magazine with the new rules and guidelines and this last paragraph: "If *Gun Dog* readers have any suggestions about these rules and guidelines, we'd be happy to hear from you."

WOW! The mailman had to use a cart.

An Organization Is Born

The timing was right. From the readership response it was clear that there was a need for some sort of an organization for the hunter and his dog. What a dilemma this produced! Who was going to do it? How does such a thing get done? Where does the money come from? Who does the work? And hundreds of other organizational questions. The magazine was a struggling new venture—it couldn't take on such a chore. For the next eight months nothing more was written on the matter in *Gun Dog.* But the letters, some *demanding* we do something, kept coming in.

During those months, behind the scenes, the activity was at a frenzied pace. It had started with G. Ray Arnett, hunter and old-line retriever trialer, who at that time was assistant secretary in President Reagan's Department of Interior. In a very dramatic and insistent manner, he argued with this writer that it was my responsibility and I must start a hunting retriever organization. I refused, saying that as a writer I had no knowledge of how to start or run a national organization. "All you do is put a board of directors together and they do the work," he claimed. I demurred. He got adamant and said, "You writers are all alike. You give us ideas, then you cop out!"

Angered by that, I got up from the lunch table, went to the phone, and called lawyer Ned Spear in Vermont. I told him that we were going to start a hunting retriever organization and he was going to be the president. Before I could say, "Don't you cop out on me!" he replied, "Fine. Let's go!"

The line-up after the first year was Ned Spear, Vermont, president; Richard A. Wolters, New York, vice-president; Omar Driskall, Louisiana, treasurer; John Krupp, Vermont, secretary; board members—David Maynard, New York; David Follansbee, New York; Jack Jagoda, Virginia; Kent

NAHRA is born. This was an early organizational meeting with the NAHRA board and the AKC. *(Author Photo)*

Repka, New York; Louis Brothers, Virginia. The board was a bunch of hunters who had no idea of the frustrations and heartache ahead.

To get started, Dave Meisner of *Gun Dog* lent the group five thousand dollars. The board believed so much in what they were creating that they each signed a note for the money. They selected a name, the North American Hunting Retriever Association (NAHRA). The first major task was to write the running rules and judges' guidelines. It was long, hard work but done so well that it has never been rewritten except for a few minor changes in words and sentence structures for clarity.

It was David Follansbee who had the foresight and convinced the board that the whole structure should be noncompetitive. The organizational and scoring systems were debated and worked out. The toughest part for the board was to forget what they knew about the established field trials and create a new game that would serve the new purpose. What was that purpose? (1) a trained hunting retriever for conservation; (2) a hunter who knew how to train a hunting dog; (3) most important: a national gene pool of working hunting stock to preserve the retriever's hunting ability!

Dogs work for points toward titles in three categories: Started, Intermediate, and Senior. Age has nothing to do with it. It depends on ability and degree of training. A dog and handler work up through the ranks.

For the first time in retriever trials, a noncompetitive system was established. Dogs did not compete against dogs to win placements. (In licensed field trials, as stated before, judges had to make the tests harder and harder as the dogs got better, in order to find the winners. This diverted the game from hunting.) Instead, with the new testing, dogs competed against a written hunting standard, which will never have to change. These are strictly hunting tests. The judges score a dog's work, and a passing grade is 80 percent. If a dog passes all the tests in its category, it is awarded points toward its title.

The NAHRA program is a simple, straightforward system with an interesting by-product. With competition out of the game, everyone is willing to help the next guy and all root for the dogs. The winner here is the dog.

The NAHRA system was well thought out. The Started dog was to display natural retrieving ability on land and water. Points were accumulated toward a Started certificate. The Intermediate dog worked toward a title of Working Retriever (WR) in both upland and waterfowl work. This dog had enough training not to embarrass a hunter on any kind of game in any part of North America. The Senior dog worked for points toward the title of Master Hunting Retriever (MHR). The MHR dog could run for Grand Master Hunting Retriever. This is the top of the line. These titles, WR, MHR, and GMHR, go on the dog's pedigree.

The NAHRA board sat at meeting after meeting brainstorming every contingency in the program—not just running rules but every facet of organizational matters. They put it all together, then were ready to announce the program.

At the first announcement, the United Kennel Club, a privately owned U.S. dog registry, contacted NAHRA and offered to sponsor our program. After two meetings, their offer was declined, for three reasons: (1) the retrievers for sixty years have been registered with the AKC, and NAHRA thought it would be a disservice to the dogs to split their registry; (2) the working plan UKC offered would leave NAHRA with no running capital, the money generated would go mostly to the UKC; and (3) they had no special experience with the retriever breeds and no retriever clubs to use as a nucleus.

Later, however, the UKC started hunting retriever tests of its own, with rules quite similar to NAHRA's.

At a luncheon meeting, the president of the AKC expressed definite interest in the NAHRA program, and eventually an agreement was reached for the two organizations to work together. Differences arose, however, over the degree of autonomy that NAHRA would have within the club, and which organization should hold the copyright to the body of rules and regulations that had been carefully drawn up by the NAHRA board. The two organizations therefore separated, and NAHRA resumed conducting its program of tests and certification of dogs independently.

The AKC administration had sold its board of directors on this new hunting testing concept in order to get NAHRA to join them. Then, with the separation and with NAHRA, which had been running things, out of the picture, they had to get their own program going—but fast. When they were forced to stop using the NAHRA rules, they wrote rules of their own that seem to satisfy them.

But the AKC faces a problem that disturbed the NAHRA board when they were together. The growth in popularity of these dogs has been almost explosive. In 1964, when the book *Water Dog* was published, 10,300 Labradors and 3,990 Goldens were registered. That put them in thirteenth and twenty-sixth places respectively; they had a combined total of 14,290 registrations. The latest figures, for 1988, put the Labrador in second place, with 86,000 dogs, and the Golden in fourth place, with 63,000, for a combined total of 149,000 dogs. That's more than 10 times the 1964 total. In the last half dozen years, the growth has been astonishing—about 10 percent a year.

All three organizations are keeping records of the dogs that successfully achieve their titles. NAHRA and the AKC have clubs coast to coast. For example, if you live in Alaska, NAHRA's computer can supply you with names and addresses of proven dogs in that state for breeding. When the testing movement started, the top hunting dog stock came from the licensed AKC field trials. Now the hunters, through these organizations, are developing their own dogs and not depending on the licensed field-trial dog. Needless to say, dogs from the show ring are out of the question. Kennels specializing in working, hunting stock are springing up all over the country.

The whole purpose of NAHRA is coming to fruition. No longer is there a fear that the Labradors will disappear from the field as the Cocker, the Poodle, the Irish Setter, and the AKC English Setter did before them.

The future hunting gene pool *(Becky Mills Photo)*

NAHRA has come up with a registry neither of the other organizations can match, because they don't recognize any registry except their own. When a dog receives its NAHRA Master Hunting Retriever title, it will be given a pedigree that shows its complete *working awards,* be they American Kennel Club, United Kennel Club, or North American Hunting Retriever Association awards. This will be the dog's complete pedigree, showing its working ability, not just the pedigree of one of these registries.

What is the hunter's responsibility? Now that we can get the hunting stock, puppies have to be better trained and dogs have to be tested so the good ones get into the working, hunting gene pool for the future.

7

Training and Where It Starts

Training a dog to be a working hunter is something the average person, with an average dog from working stock, can accomplish with quick and astonishing results.

There are two basic problems with the uninitiated, and they are both cop-outs. The first is the hunter who says that his dog, which he always claims is great, does everything he wants his dog to do. On close examination of that, we can almost hear this story or one very similar repeated many times over: "My dog was great! He retrieved six birds before we had time to even get settled in the blind."

Go hunting with that guy and here is what you will find: The dog is not trained. He has terrible manners, wants to lick everyone's face, eat their sandwiches, and is not steady—which means he does not wait to be sent for the downed birds but charges through the shooters on first shot to get out of the blind in order to get that bird: a dangerous, unsafe practice.

Yes, he did make six retrieves at sunup, but the dog made those retrieves in spite of the hunter and the training he gave his dog. The dog's mommy and daddy gave him the instinct to retrieve, so when the guns dropped the birds in the decoys it took no training on the hunter's part to get the dog to make the retrieves. In fact, if more birds were coming in, the hunter could not have stopped the dog from crashing out of the blind and flaring the incoming birds. If some of the birds fell on land behind the blind, the hunter might have no problem walking the dog through the cover telling the dog to hunt 'em up. The dog *may* find the birds because of the hunting nose that came with him at birth. A great dog? For that kind of retrieving, a dog isn't a real necessity. The birds in the decoys and behind the blind could have been picked up by the hunter during a lull in the shooting.

One of the real needs for a trained dog is to recover the birds that are wounded, fly off a hundred yards or more, and then fall out of the sky onto water or land. Wounded birds will crawl to a hiding place to die. Since, in most cases, the dog sits on the floor of the blind, he does not see these winged birds go down, so they become "blind" retrieves. For conservation reasons, these are the birds that must be recovered for the table. If they are not brought to the hunter's bag, the hunter by law has a right to shoot another bird—or keep shooting them until he has his limit. Wounded birds not recovered die and are a waste. There is no way an untrained dog can recover a winged bird when it did not see the fall "into that marsh across the water." This is where the handling work that Dave Elliot introduced in the early 1930s becomes so important in our American hunting.

The hunter who takes his untrained dog into the field boasting and claiming that his dog does everything he wants or needs is not squarely facing the problems of hunting. But how many times have we been in the blind with such a dog? And the owner of such a dog does not seem to realize how his dog ruins things for the well-trained dog.

When the NAHRA program started, G. Ray Arnett, then the assistant secretary of the Department of the Interior, had a dream: "Wouldn't it be great if every hunting party was required to have a proven working retriever?" Such a program would save as many ducks a year as Ducks Unlimited does. But there is a sad commentary to such a dream.

A dedicated duck-hunting buddy in Vermont won in a lottery the right to go into a federal sanctuary and hunt from an assigned blind that the government provided. This had always been touted to him as the best mallard shooting in the state. As he tells the story, he loaded the car the night before, laid his hunting gear and clothes out, and went to bed at 8:00 P.M. after he tucked the kids in. He was so excited that he didn't sleep and at 2:00 A.M. turned the alarm off before it went off. Up and at 'em he dressed, grabbed a fast breakfast, put Old Six Pack, his trusty Lab, in his kennel in the back of his four-by-four vehicle, then drove off to pick up his buddy. At 4:00 A.M. they arrived on time at the sanctuary.

They were assigned a blind and given a map to show them how to get to it. Under the map in big bold print was the shocker: NO DOGS ALLOWED. Thinking this meant Poodles or some such, he asked the game warden in charge what it meant. The answer was just what it says. No dogs. My friend tried to explain that he had a *trained* hunting retriever. The warden answered, "Mister, I'm sorry, but we have heard that story for years. Everyone says their dog is good. But they have caused such out-of-control problems that we have had to ban all dogs. Guys running around, blowing whistles and screaming at their dogs, have ruined the shooting for all others in the area." Terribly disappointed, my friend and Old Six Pack drove home in time for a second breakfast. But what a sad state of retriever affairs!

So the hunter's first cop-out is asking too little of our retrievers. Most hunters do not know how to train to get any more out of the dog than what the dog brings naturally to the hunter.

The second cop-out is "Oh, I don't have the patience or the time to train a dog." First of all, patience is not the problem with average people.

The sport of training retrievers is becoming a game unto itself. It's good outdoor fun, and more and more people are taking the time to train their dogs. *(Author Photo)*

They are confusing patience with frustration because of not knowing what to do. There is a simple, step-by-step training way to go that 99.44 percent of the time won't fail. If the hunter does not know the way and things go wrong, he gets frustrated, but that is not having no patience.

What about the time cop-out? As a young pup, from seven weeks to four months, ten or fifteen minutes a day broken down into five-minute training sessions will do the job. Oh, yes, plus as much time for play as possible. Surely that amount of time can be fitted into even a busy schedule. Twenty minutes or so of work, three times a week, from five months old to a year, will make a hunting dog. Once it learns these lessons it won't forget them, and you will have a fine hunting companion for the next ten years. Again, it's knowing that step-by-step procedure. If you can read, you can learn it. My book *Game Dog* goes step by step and so do some others.

A New Kind of Training

The original concept of the hunting testing program for retrievers deliberately set out to educate the hunter and his dog. It's a startling revelation to look back, even these few years, and see the dramatic improvement in the dogs who have been in the program and the young dogs that have come up through the NAHRA tests. Yet there was one thing that was not seriously taken into account back at the beginning of the movement, a by-product of the game: that's the social aspect, the fun of the events, the informal training sessions, the people, dogs, and guns. Although this is true for almost any sport that brings people together, in this case it was something new for the hunter, who has traditionally been a loner, hunting year after year in his specific areas with his cronies. That's one reason the average hunter's dog was not a very good working animal. The hunter often spent a lifetime in his sport, yet never saw a well-trained dog work. As B. Waters said at the beginning of the century, "The hunter had too low a standard for his dog and for himself." Getting a dialogue started among the hunting fraternity did more for the development of the dogs than any other single factor.

Hunters brought their dogs from all over a region to participate in the new field tests. About NAHRA's first licensed event, Joe May of the James River Club in Virginia recalled, "We never knew we had so many retrievers in the area. . . . They came out from behind the trees . . . out of the woodwork!" With them came ideas on how-to and how-not-to train and handle dogs. Right or wrong ideas were disseminated, and the little guy learned a lot by listening and seeing dogs work.

The professional dog trainer got into the act. Almost from the inception of the new hunting retriever movement there was a place for the professional. Many of the pros' dogs did exceptional jobs, and it was the first time many of the hunters had seen what a hunting dog could do and is supposed to do. Many of the pros were willing to help all comers, to talk and give advice, because the pro himself wanted the new movement to succeed in his area and in the surrounding clubs. Since most clubs can only handle at the most two licensed events in a year, two tests wouldn't add up to much of a program. For such a movement to be successful, a series of clubs within half a day's drive of each other is necessary. The whole idea is to get many clubs going within a region so a testing "circuit" can be formed in order to get as many events running each year as possible. Dogs are awarded titles on the number of times they pass the written standard. The more events they enter, the faster the titles can be earned.

While the AKC and the UKC were boasting high numbers of dogs passing their tests, in the NAHRA program that first year only a handful of dogs earned titles. NAHRA's concept was and still is to get the dogs up to the standard, not the standard down to the dogs.

THE NEW PROGRAM

At the very beginning of the program, it appeared as though a problem might develop. While the new concept looked good on paper and when first announced in the pages of *Gun Dog* magazine, there was still an old field-trial taboo that had to be overcome. The hunter, without even knowing much about field trials, had an aversion to them. Since the AKC, for half a century, had made no place in its program for the hunter, almost without knowing why, the hunter had a disdainful opinion of the AKC and of field trials in general. And those hunters that did get interested were turned off by the expense, politics, and kind of training necessary for AKC-licensed trials. At first they saw NAHRA as just another field-trial outfit. Although they looked alike, because the setup and the same "tools" of field trials were used—judges, birds, bird boys to throw, guns, fields, water, and dogs—once the hunters saw the way they were used and realized that the NAHRA tests were based on real hunting tests, they became interested and then hooked.

With the hunting program less than five years old, there are now two well-trained retrievers in America, the field-trial dog and the hunter's dog. Those who have taken part in the new program now have well-trained working retrievers.

There are always "people" problems in organized movements. The original licensed field trials certainly showed that and so did the hunter's testing program. Games people play get very political, and the new hunting testing movement, just like the older licensed field trials, is a game. The saving grace with the new game is that the dog work won't change. Politics won't get into that as it did in the licensed AKC trials. The written standard will keep the dog work from getting out of hand, but there is still one problem and that's to keep the new game within the cost of what the hunter can spend.

There Are Two Ways to Train a Retriever: The Natural and Force Methods

To be facetious one could say there are three ways to train a retriever, if we add to the list what most hunters do: let the dog do it itself working strictly from instinct. But as we have said, this produces unsatisfactory results. You don't get a trained animal without work. There is no other way: time in means results out.

In today's licensed field trials, force training is used because of the required training precision necessary and the difficulty of the tests. Their events have become unbelievable tests of obedience. Although some in the hunting program are now using the force system, with a well-bred dog it is not necessary, and excellent results, for the hunter, can be obtained by the natural method.

First, it must be understood that there is force used in *both* methods.

There is no such thing as training without force: it's only a matter of degree.

The force system uses the ear pinch as the main tool in teaching and then goes on to the electric collar to fine-tune the training by punishing or threatening to punish the dog for its mistakes, *once the dog is trained* and knows what it should do but instead does wrong. The tools of force will be discussed later, but it must be stated at the outset that cruelty is not part of the force training.

The natural system could take longer to get the dog trained to its advance work, but it does the job. It uses a choke collar, a strap, a commanding voice and commanding attitude with a lot of repetition—oh yes, and being fast on one's feet is important so that the reprimand can be given as soon after the mistake happens as possible. The advantage of the force and collar system is that the reprimand can be delivered the exact second it is needed.

The natural method takes less force and is the best system for the beginning trainer and the hunter. By starting with a pup before it has learned any bad habits, the hunter can train the pup as it grows. It's a step-by-step learning process that starts with the simple beginning commands and builds on them. Start a dog late, and you are going to have to undo many of the things the dog has already learned, and that "ain't" easy.

The natural method trainer should understand that the young pup's brain is like a sponge and can and will absorb information at an unbelievable rate. Dogs, just like humans, lose that "crash learning" ability as they mature. You try to learn a new language at age thirty-five and see how long it takes and what results you get, yet a child just out of diapers has already learned a language and understands it all. The young dog is going to learn no matter what its situation. The important thing for the trainer is to take advantage of the "sponge phase" of the mental development of a pup and make sure it's what *you* want the dog to learn, not what *it* wants.

The COME command is a good example to explain how the natural method works and just what kind of force is involved. This COME command is where trainers first get into trouble.

What the novice trainer usually says is that the pup knows its SIT, STAY, COME commands, except that if it is off running in a field, then it won't come. Or it knows SIT, STAY unless it hears a gun go off; then it's off a-runnin'. The problem is there are no ifs or buts, no exceptions to the rules. How do you get this "no exception" to the rules with the natural training method?

The answer is right there in front of the trainer's nose: never let the dog make a mistake without correcting it right on the spot. First, you never make a request of a dog—you command a dog. When you give a dog an order, the dog has two things it can learn: (1) I better do it or there is going to be trouble; (2) I'll do it as and when I please because the boss is a patsy.

When the training starts at seven weeks and on through to the end of the mental development period at sixteen weeks, the pup is easy to handle because you can outrun it.

Usually, if these early lessons are done correctly, you will have little trouble as the dog matures. But the dog will enter that adolescent phase of development at about the seventeenth to twentieth week, as the animal behaviorists tell us, and it will start to test you. The dog is smart enough to know that the best command to test the trainer on is COME. After all, the SIT command is usually given when the trainer and dog are close together. The dog soon realizes that it has four legs and that you only have two. "What are you going to do about it if I don't come?" The answer is simple: with strap in hand, you will have to run the dog down. Then you will use the strap across the flank and speak firmly while hovering over the dog. You are going to have to be a little ugly! You are going to teach the dog what the strap is for. You are going to have to teach the dog that you are not its friend if it acts like that.

Okay, what does all this mean? Once the dog learns that the strap can sting and that you will use it, it learns that you mean business—you are not a patsy—and to get back on your good side all it has to do is obey. Remember, almost all breeds of retrievers come with an extremely highly developed desire to please. The strap does not have to be used in all disobedience situations. Once the dog learns what the strap can do, the harshness of your voice and the threatening attitude of your standing over the dog with a raised strap will be enough in most cases to fold the dog and make it submissive.

You have to be consistent! A young dog will constantly be looking for a crack in your armor. If you give a COME command and then do not follow up on it, I can just see the dog smiling to itself. Running a dog down can get into the realm of coronary problems. It's suggested that a fenced-in field be used to make it easier to corner the dog.

In the natural system, it is important that the trainer understands what the dog understands. Dogs do not learn our language as such. They learn by rote that a certain sound means a certain response is required. They do not understand sentences. The dog learns to read you. It can tell by your stance, your body language, your smell, and especially the tone of your voice what your mood or your attitude toward it is.

A good example of this took place working with a friend and his dog. The dog was a young, tough "high roller." He loved to retrieve, but once out in the field on his own he'd give the handler the "thumb." He was unruly. He loved to run, and he had learned that his master could do nothing about it. He was spanked so much that I do believe that he considered the spanking part of the game of retrieve. The spanking rolled off his back, and he was just as eager to continue after the spanking—nothing fazed him. Finally we made a plan. The dog refused to come on whistle, yet we knew from his yard training that he absolutely knew the command. The handler was sent out to run down and corner the dog, blowing the COME command as he went. He finally tackled the dodging dog. The handler got on top of the dog and put his forearm on the dog's neck. He held the dog to the ground and put his own head against the dog's head. The handler was breathing hard from all the running. The dog was held down. The more he struggled the harder he was held. Very shortly the dog lay still. The struggle was over, and he had given up. This was body language the dog knew innately. The pressure at the dog's neck was used by the dominant animal in a wolf pack to teach any male who questioned his authority who the boss was. The questioner was in a bad position to start a fight, and if he were smart, he would submit. That's body language, and it worked. The high roller all of a sudden started to obey the whistle.

In the natural training method, we are depending on the dog's natural tendency to please, but a dog must learn what reprimand is and know that it will be used if need be. The question is always asked, "How much?" The answer is, not too much or too little. A good trainer "reads" his dog and learns what will do the trick.

One of the big problems with this natural method is getting to the dog and reprimanding it before it forgets what it did wrong.

PRAISE TO TRAIN; REMOVE IT TO WORK

We teach and show a dog what we want by using praise. Once the dog understands what we want and is responding to the command, then the praise is gradually removed. It is used for teaching. When the command is learned, the work becomes the dog's satisfaction and reward. We praise a young dog for making the retrieve. We let it know that is what we want. A dog who has learned that will strut back very pleased with itself with its bird—it has gotten its reward, the retrieve.

Praise releases a dog from being under your command. We tell a young dog to SIT and praise it for doing so. Then we repeat the command and tell it just how good it is and pat it and make a fuss over it. It loves that and responds with a few licks on the face to tell you it likes you too. Then we command SIT again and go through the routine until it learns the command. Then the fuss has to be cut out. Try that with a dog who knows what the command means, and when you praise it it will respond by getting up thinking it's fuss time. My Tar, in such a situation, will jump up to give my face a lick before he is off on his own looking for lady smells.

With these tools of understanding the dog, we then use the most important one in the natural training method, and that is repetition— consistent repetition. Always do the job the same way, use the same commands, same body language, taking the dog step by step through the training.

To summarize the natural training method: We start at a very early age with no force used at all. The dog learns its basic commands this way at that early age. If it makes a mistake, it is made to do it again until it does it right. It is like play but doing it over is the force.

As the dog gets older, a stern voice can be added to the training. The stern voice becomes the force.

Once the dog is old enough to receive a mild spanking for not obeying (about age four months), the spanking becomes the force. The threat of spanking and the threat of your displeasure using voice and body gestures become the force. The dog must be kept "off balance," not knowing if the strap will be used or not. The handler will find that voice and attitude will be enough in most cases to get the point across and that the spanking is saved for serious violations.

ELECTRICITY—SPACE-AGE TRAINING

The use of the electric collar will be discussed in an overall way in some detail. As we have said before, this training section will not be comprehensive, because I have already produced books on the natural training method.

But no book has come on the market to give the hunter a basic understanding of the electric collar.

If there was ever a training tool that has been misunderstood by some who use it and the general dog public, it is the electric collar—electronic collar—shock collar—or just "collar," whichever you prefer. The way some people used it when it was introduced brought to mind the electric chair. Yet the same tool in the hands of other trainers became the most humane method of training a dog.

The first collars did one job, delivered a shock to the dog. The handler carried a transmitter, and the dog wore a receiver on its collar. In the early days of the collar, it was used for punishment alone. If the dog made a mistake or paid no attention to the handler, it was zapped, "burned." Here is an example of that early use. The transmitter had the power to reach out hundreds of yards so a working retriever had no place to "hide"—it was always within range. If a handler whistled for the dog to SIT when it was 150 yards away and the dog ignored him, it was punished right there on the spot, instantly. It received a shock and in most cases cried out in pain. Without the collar, in that same situation where the dog did not obey the SIT command, the handler had to run out that 150 yards and, if he could catch the dog, reprimand it with a strap. But by the time the handler got out to the dog, the dog had most likely forgotten what it had done wrong. Instantaneous reprimand made the training easier and made a lot of sense, but it had its problems—overuse could ruin a dog.

The collar makes training in the advanced work much faster. This is important to the professional and the field trialer because the owner always wants to have a dog in the competition or coming up through the ranks. Otherwise, he is out of the game until he has a dog to run. Speed in learning becomes important. Also, it costs a lot of money to obtain the kind of precision training needed for field trials. Speed in training saves money.

Some dogs could not handle this kind of shock treatment and were washed out of the program. Some dogs managed but did their job reluctantly, as if they were constantly looking over their shoulders. They were always afraid of making a mistake and did their job with their tails down. In the early days, you could watch a dog run a test and tell if he had been collar trained. Of course, they all were not like that. Many were "tough" enough to stand up to the shock treatment and do their job with outstanding skill.

With experience, the professional soon learned to handle the new tool better. First, the collar is not used to train the dog. The training has to be done the conventional way so that the dog knows the commands before the collar is used. The collar is only used for corrections once the dog knows what it is supposed to do. So the collar adds a lot of extra work in the early training, but speeds up the advanced work later.

We will explain later, but the dog has to be conditioned to the collar before it is used in the field. You will surely confuse a dog if he is taken to the field and zapped when something goes wrong. Conditioning is done in yard training. But if the collar is used in anger or out of frustration, the dog can be ruined very quickly: it just gives up. On the other hand, reprimanding the dog the instant it makes a mistake teaches the dog to pay attention and not to make the same mistake twice. There is a very fine line in all of this, and many new users of the collar failed because they believed the collar would solve the training problem that they could not handle normally. The collar received a bad name and was considered a tool for the advanced amateur and the pro—and even they could make mistakes.

Much research has been done by the manufacturers. Tritronics, the first company in this field, needed all the input it could get and used animal behaviorists, professional trainers, advanced amateurs, and hunters as sources. The answer was there, but it had to be understood and technical advancements made. Today the equipment is very sophisticated, and so is

The electric collar received a bad name at first, but with a lot of study and understanding, it can be the most humane way to train. *(Author Photo)*

the method of using it. What was once a tool for the professional, and not the average hunter, is now for any intelligent trainer.

The most advanced collar is the Tritronics Pro 100. The transmitter is long-range and *can do many things*. It can send the same command as the original collar that shocks the dog for punishment, but that has become a minor part of its use. It now has a variable intensity that can be regulated at the handler's fingertips, from very weak to intense. The weak shock, or tickle, becomes a reminder to the dog to pay attention. The transmitter can, at fingertip control, also send an audio warning buzz to the dog that the shock is coming within a second—pay attention fast! It can be set to give only the buzz that reminds the dog to pay attention. Then, when all goes well, it can also give an electronic sound that the dog learns to associate with "That's a good fellow. You are doing fine." It's a new way to talk to your dog while one hundred yards away.

Now the trainer has a whole bag of tricks to use. The dog is conditioned to the collar in the yard training on all the basic commands that it had already learned as a small pup. Now it goes through the same program again, but this time with the collar. The collar, which has a box attached to it, is something new for the dog, so it is conditioned to it, too. A dummy collar, the same shape and weight, but without the electronics, is worn around the house a few hours, off and on, each day so the dog becomes used to it and not upset by it and never knows when the real one is on. (Try correcting a dog who won't obey to the COME command by putting it on a long check cord and pulling it in if need be. The dog will soon learn to come just fine while it is attached to the cord. Release it and it knows you have lost control, and it'll be off on its merry way. But this is no longer true, as we shall see shortly. The rope is used to teach the dog what we want, and when the line is removed, we still have the collar control for "reaching" the dog.)

Now the trainer has at his fingertips a whole new bag of tricks. Using a low intensity so the dog does not feel enough pain to cry out, you command SIT. It knows what to do because it has learned the command. If it is slow responding, give it a nick with the juice. It'll look startled but respond. As soon as it starts to make the motion to sit, the electricity is cut off. Timing becomes very important. You can then give the dog the electronic "good boy" sound at a distance, which is like a pat or praise. Shortly you will see it wag its tail at the "good boy" sound. It gives the dog confidence.

Once the dog gets shocked, it will obviously try to avoid it, although it does not understand where the shock comes from. Here is where the buzz and shock system come into use. The dog soon learns that the buzz is the warning before the shock. If it complies quickly with the command, it will avoid the discomfort. It can turn off the buzz, and that means no shock. In one of the transmitter modes, the buzz lasts for less than a second; then the shock automatically follows. It won't take much for the dog to learn that when it hears the buzz, if it obeys immediately, it will escape the shock.

With the new collars, the handler has at his fingertips a means of allowing the punishment to fit the crime. There are now many options. If the dog is 150 yards off, you can "talk" to it as if you were there with it. On the whistle command to SIT, if it does it, you can immediately give it the "good boy" sound. If the dog hesitates and does not respond quickly enough, give it the buzzer, which will remind it of what is next: the shock. If it is still hesitant, it gets zapped lightly. If the dog gives you the thumb, and you know it knows better, you can increase the shock and give it the "chair." What you are doing is teaching the dog to avoid trouble at the exact instant it is needed. It learns to respond quickly, which is very difficult to instill in some dogs when they are a distance from you.

Dogs trained by this avoidance system will learn to work quickly. They won't have the fear, built into the early collar use, of being burned at every infraction of the law. They know the quicker they do the job, the safer they will be, and if they do a good job, the "good boy" buzz will be their reward. Once the dog is trained, it is weaned away from the collar. If it slips it will be put back on, but most of the time the dummy collar will keep it "safe."

Avoidance and escape training are part of a whole new ball game for the hunter. Previous to this new equipment, the collar was something for the average hunter to avoid. Now he's got a good tool, but he must go slowly and must learn the new psychology of electronic training. This is a humane way to train. Screaming and beating and running after a dog get little accomplished—except high blood pressure.

Now the licensed field-trial people can put away the tools they never did like talking about: the slingshots, BB guns, air pistols, and shotguns loaded with bird shot.

FORCE TRAINING BY THE MASTER

It was the professional trainer who developed the force-training method in this country. The results have been spectacular. In the licensed field-trial

Bachman Doar, one of the highly respected professional retriever trainers in this country *(Author Photo)*

game, the amateur trainer has learned the force system and is now as good as the professional as a trainer and handler. But force training is almost a science. It must be understood. The electric collar is a powerful tool and *is not used to train the dog; it is used to reinforce the training the dog has already had.* It is best to think of it as a reminder to the dog that it is about to get into trouble or is in trouble.

For example, for the person who buys a collar to correct a dog who won't stop on the whistle in the field, and believes he can "burn" the dog to make it stop, it's guaranteed he will ruin his dog! If you lose your temper while training with a collar, you will ruin your dog!

One of the best exponents today of force training, and on into the collar work, is Bachman Doar of Virginia and South Carolina. I like the idea of Bach's being the spokesman for the force-training method in this book for a number of reasons. First, his credentials are top drawer and worth repeating. He has won the American National with Super Nova Chief and the Canadian National twice and has produced fifteen or so field-trial champions. But the reason Bach is a perfect spokesman for the force-training method is that he is known in dog circles as a very gentle man. The image in England and many other countries is that a trainer who uses the electric collar is a monster. Some countries such as South Africa, of all places, prohibit the use of the collar. Bach is a good spokesman because he has been a professional trainer for fifteen years and is a well-educated gentleman who just does not fit the monster role.

Bach started using the force method when years ago a client sent him a problem dog for training. The dog had been an exceptionally good hunter but now refused to retrieve anything ever since it had had a serious encounter with a wounded goose and was slapped around. Using his natural method of repeatedly putting the dummy in the dog's mouth and commanding HOLD just wouldn't work on this dog. It looked as if this dog had had it! Nothing seemed to work to get the dog interested in retrieving again. The natural method was not going to work. There was only one thing left to try to save the dog, and that was the ear-pinch force training.

Bach used the Charlie Morgan ear-pinch method that was written up in the Morgan book by D. L. and Ann Walters. It went so well and was so easy to do on this problem dog, that Bach decided to start all his dogs with the force method. It made them surefire retrievers, and they would never refuse to retrieve, having been trained this way.

Bach explained how he got the problem dog back to retrieving geese. First he used a wooden dumbbell. When he pinched the dog's ear, the dog

The ear pinch almost elicits a reflex response. Pinch the ear and the mouth opens. The ear pinch will make the dog a dependable, surefire retriever. *(Author Photo)*

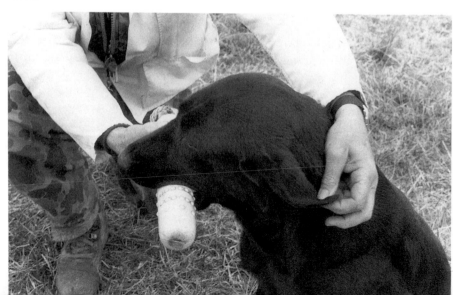

opened his mouth because of the pain and the dumbbell was inserted into the dog's mouth as the command FETCH was given. The instant the dog's mouth opened, the thumb pinch was released. Look at it this way: if someone pinched you, your first response would be to open your mouth, suck in air, and say, "OW!" It's an easy way to get the mouth open without prying, and then in goes the dumbbell.

In very short order, the dog opens its mouth, almost like a reflex response, when its ear is pinched. The dumbbell is inserted and the command FETCH given. The dog quickly learns that the ear pinch stops as soon as it opens its mouth and takes the dumbbell. Then the operation is repeated, and instead of putting the dumbbell at the dog's mouth, the trainer places it a few inches in front of the dog's mouth so the dog has to reach for it. As soon as the dog opens its mouth to start the retrieve, the ear pressure is stopped. Next the dog has to lean over and pick the dumbbell off the floor. Then the dumbbell is placed a step or so in front of the dog. The wooden dumbbell is good to use because of its shape, the dog can easily pick it up by the bar. The other reason to use the dumbbell instead of a dummy is so the dog will not associate the discomfort of this learning procedure with the dummy that will be the main training tool later.

This was the training corrective procedure Bach gave the problem dog who refused to retrieve. Once the dog got the idea and was responding well, dummies were substituted for the dumbbell. Then dead birds were used, then live birds. The dog that once had refused to retrieve anything was given Muscovy ducks to simulate the weight of the goose. Gradually, the problem dog was brought around and was back in the goose blind the next season. The result was so successful that Bach has force-trained all his dogs since that first experience.

Everyone seems to think that the force method is a shortcut to retriever training. Bach disagrees, saying that it is not a shortcut and that it actually takes longer because there are more initial training steps to include in the early training.

What the force-training method plus the collar will do is speed up the advanced work the dog will be taught toward the end of its schooling—the fine-tuning to finish it off, especially in the work of lining and blind retrieves.

Bach says that in all training the first thing to learn is SIT, STAY, COME. It is taught the conventional way. It is not until these commands are learned—*really* learned—that the force system is started. Under normal circumstances, this force method will start when the pup is about six or seven months.

The pup is started on the dumbbell after its adult teeth have come in. The ear-pinch method is used and the command is FETCH. Once the dog has the dumbbell in its mouth, the command HOLD is given and the trainer taps the dog under the jowl as the HOLD command is repeated. HOLD is combined with HEEL, and the pup learns to walk and never drop or spit out the dummy until the new command DROP is given. Bach repeats the HOLD command at heel with the dumbbell until the dog understands what he is after; then he substitutes a canvas dummy, then a plastic dummy, and finishes off with a goose wing.

Step by step, the distance of the FETCH command is increased. It starts out by placing the dummy in the open mouth. Next the dog has to reach or stretch for it. Then the dog has to bend to the floor to get hold of the dummy. Once the dummy is on the floor, it is gradually placed farther and farther away across the floor. The FETCH command has turned from initiating first a reflex response to open the mouth and take the object to now meaning that the dog should make a retrieve. At the same time the dog learns the HOLD command.

The word *fetch* will be dropped as soon as the dog learns that FETCH means to go pick the object up and hold it. After that is learned, the command will be changed to whatever the handler wants to use in the field to send his dog: example, the word *back,* or two blasts on the whistle as I do, or some handlers like to use the dog's name to send it.

Bach insists that timing is important. The pinch is given and the release comes the instant the dog opens its mouth to take hold of the object. This is done with the dummies and goose wing, and then when it is done in the field, first dead birds are used, then live birds.

If a dog becomes reluctant in the field, it might have to be taken—by the ear—all the way to the thrown dummy. Actually, according to Bach, this is something that won't happen very often because now is the time the electric collar will be used in conjunction with the FETCH command.

But first here is how Bach uses the collar. After a young dog has been yard-trained to SIT, STAY, COME by the conventional system, it is introduced to the electric collar. There are five degrees of shock. Number 1 is the weakest and 5 is the strongest. Bach will use a number 2, which is not very strong. He will start by reteaching the command COME with the collar. The dog has been trained on a long lead rope to come when called. After the dog does this well, it is given the command COME, given a reminder tug on the lead and also a short "tap" with the electric collar. If the dog stops, it is given a reminder with a tug on the rope and another tap with the collar. Soon the rope is dropped, and a tap with the collar itself will do the trick and the dog will come to you directly. So the dog has now been introduced to the collar.

After the ear pinch, force training is almost completed. The collar is introduced into the force-fetch at the last stages of the FETCH command. The dog is sent by voice and ear pinch a short distance, five or ten yards, to make the retrieve. The dog knows the command FETCH, and the ear pinch is used in conjunction with the command to send the dog that short distance to make the retrieve. Once the dog does this, the shock of the collar is added, and then the ear pinch is stopped. You have now substituted the collar for the ear pinch. This is the start of the conversion that will allow the trainer to work with the dog hundreds of yards away. As Bach says, "You can't pinch a dog's ear a hundred yards away."

Bach says that, if you can teach the dog to come back on a straight line to you on a retrieve, it will then be easy to teach it to go out on a straight line to make the retrieve. This means that on returning from making a retrieve the dog will come on a straight line directly to you. He will not *run the bank* (run around the body of water) but will swim back to you. This is the first step in teaching the dog to *take a line* (go out to make a retrieve by following the handler's hand). Bach starts the COME command to introduce the dog to the electric collar. He does this by using a long line, or check cord, the whistle, and the collar. The dog is brought in on the COME command, directly across small bodies of water with a little tug on the line and the whistle. If it deviates, the dog will get a "reminder" with the collar. The dog learns not to run the bank. Once this is learned, the reverse will work: the dog knows to make a direct run for the dummy with no deviation. By repetition of this, the dog learns to run in straight lines, follow the hand that directs it to the fall—the first step in taking a line for a blind retrieve.

One of the reasons that the collar has received a bad name is that the forcing is often made much tougher than the system Bach uses. He obviously gets the work out of the dog without killing the dog's spirit. Dogs that he trains from "scratch" run with their tails high, the sign of a happy dog. It is not so much a question of how high the electric charge is, as of the timing of when it is given.

Bach divides the use of the collar into two categories. One is force training, which we have just discussed, and the other is enforcing. *Enforcing* is done after the dog has been through its training and knows its commands but decides when it is a hundred yards or so out in the field that it is going to do things its own way. In the natural training method, you have to run that hundred yards out to your dog and reprimand it on the spot—try that in a swamp!

The way Bach handles command refusals is always from the SIT command. Bach feels the dog's thought processes are turned off while it is running, so the dog is not given a shock for punishment while it is running and doing wrong. Here is an example. On a blind retrieve, the dog refuses to take an *over* (that is, a cast to the side), but instead takes a *back* (running farther away from the handler). The dog is not given a shock with the collar as it is making the mistake of running back. Instead, the dog is immediately given a SIT command by whistle. It has done wrong, and it now knows it. While it sits and looks at the handler waiting for the next command, it is given a shock, its reproof for doing wrong. Now the dog has plenty of time to think about it. On the next command, you can bet your bottom dollar that the dog will follow orders just to avoid the shock that comes when it does wrong.

Here is where the trainer has to keep his cool. *Burning* (too high a charge and too long a shock) a dog for making a mistake is not necessary. It will kill a dog's enthusiasm, and you can see it in dogs that have been treated that way. They do not run with enthusiasm or have happy tails.

To sum up: What we have now is a training tool that can reach out to the dog at any distance and "tell" the dog that it is doing wrong. The correction is made at the exact time of the infringement, and a dog can understand that. If used properly, the force training with the ear pinch and the collar are the most humane ways of training. There is little difference between that and whipping a dog that won't obey. Reprimand is an important part of learning. Without it, children and dogs become spoiled brats. Bach says, "You can't train a field-trial dog with cookies!"

There is another technique for teaching the force method. Robert Milner in his book *Retriever Training for the Duck Hunter* (1985) describes it in detail. He puts the dog on an eight-foot table and attaches its collar to an overhead chain and pulley system. The dog can move on the table but not get off. A cord is attached to the dog's paw and then around a toe. The rope is pulled; the dog opens its mouth from the pain of the toe pull. The command FETCH is given, and the dummy or dumbbell is inserted in its mouth. It's the same principle as the ear pinch except it takes a specific place to do the training and a special apparatus to accomplish the same thing the ear pinch does.

The real disadvantage of the Milner system is that you have to take your dog back to the apparatus and rig it up in the harness and toe pull to make any correction. The ear-pinch system can be done anywhere, in the field and on the spot. It takes only a second to accomplish. And the ear pinch has another advantage. You can take the dog's ear in your hand and use a scolding voice when it does wrong and without even pinching the dog get a submissive result. Change your voice tone to your normal tone and you'll get a wag of the tail that says, "Okay, boss, let's get to work!"

In this space age, training has come a long way from the sixteenth-century method of dropping a glove and walking on, then sending the dog back to make the retrieve. This taught him to fetch and to use his nose. Instinct took care of the rest of the dog's training. Today we require so much from our American retrievers that training is a lengthy, step-by-step job. The new psychology and the advances of the electronic collar make dog training almost a science. What does all this mean for the hunter?

The decision whether or not to go the route of the electric collar should not be made just because it is available. Plenty of fine hunting retrievers have been made and are still being made using the natural system exclusively. It really has to be dealer's choice. It has been said that every good trainer has ruined a few dogs while learning to use the collar. This is not so true now as it was a few years ago. The equipment is better, and there are a lot of people using it, so more advice is available.

What NAHRA Dogs Should Know

My book *Game Dog,* using the natural training method, takes the hunter through step-by-step retriever training for both upland and waterfowl birds. It is not the purpose of this book to repeat all that training. What we will do is to explain what is necessary and what a dog should know in order to run successfully in the three categories of the NAHRA program. This will be done by referring to the highlights of the NAHRA rule book.

All three testing programs, AKC, UKC, and NAHRA, divide the dogs into three categories. They each call them by different names, but their meanings are the same. The NAHRA names were the first and clearest to understand, so they will be used here. The three categories are Started, Intermediate, and Senior. NAHRA also has a Beginner class, but we won't have much to say about it.

THE STARTED DOG

The Started dog will work more from instinct and breeding rather than obedience or training. The purpose is to bring a young or started dog along as a hunter. What we are looking for is good style, courage, and hunting potential. The judges will look for those hunting traits that are passed down to a dog from its sire and dam.

The dog will be put to very simple, basic tests that should demonstrate desire to hunt, cooperation with the hunter, and natural ability.

Here are the things that are expected of a Started dog: A Started dog is required to be steady, but the dog may be restrained so it won't break. That means, as explained before, when a bird is shot or thrown for it and a gun goes off, we would expect it to rush out and start the retrieve without being commanded to do so. To prevent this from happening, a line or cord may be placed around the dog's neck to restrain it from running out and *breaking* (being unsteady). When the command to send the dog is given by the judge, the handler releases the dog. One end of the line slips through the handler's fingers, and the dog runs free of the line. Dogs of only four months of age can be trained to be steady. It's no great trick to teach steadiness to a young dog. But if you take that chance in the Started test and do not restrain your dog with a line, if by chance it breaks, it will be dropped from further testing. There is a saving grace to all this. If the dog does break but is stopped immediately and brought back under control, the break is considered only a minor infraction.

What the judge is really looking for is the spirit or lack of it that the dog demonstrates. A lethargic dog that more or less wants to do its work is not going to make a very satisfactory hunting companion. On the other

The Started dog may be restrained from breaking with a light line through its collar. *(Becky Mills Photo)*

hand, the pup that is jumping all about, out of control, barking, displaying a wildness and hyperactivity is not what the hunter wants either.

The Started dog gets only single retrieves. There will be five of them, and they will be both on land and on water. The judge is going to ask himself, as he sees the dog work, "Would I like to have that dog?" The answer will be yes if the dog demonstrates that it really wants to make that retrieve. If it runs out with style and goes about the whole job with a happy air, its future looks good. On the other hand, if the dog runs out and then seems to forget why its handler has just spent twenty-five or so dollars for it to get into this event, there is trouble ahead. The dog that sniffs around, is a moper, drops the bird, and urinates on the next tree shows that retrieving obviously isn't one of its first desires. The judge is going to want to see more spunk and initiative than that.

Although it is not difficult to teach a Started dog to hold the bird and deliver it to hand, the test requires only that the dog deliver the bird back to within a specified radius—about ten feet.

For the Started dog the retrieves are short, seventy-five yards on land and fifty yards on water. The judge will watch to see if the dog uses its nose, stays in close to the fall, and establishes a hunt area. There is often luck in pinpointing a fall so a dog that establishes a good hunt and sticks with it could get almost as good a score as the perfect pinpoint job.

In most cases, dead or shackled birds will be thrown for the dog by bird boys who are hidden from the dog's view. There will be attention-getting devices used, such as duck calls or a *dry shot* (no bird thrown with the sound of the gun) or the boy calling before he throws the bird, "Bird in the air." After the bird is thrown, a *popper* (blank shot) will be fired when the bird is at the top of the throwing arc.

A good judge will make sure that the dog gets plenty of opportunity to figure out where the birds are coming from. Although the dog might not see the bird boys except for a brief moment while they throw the bird, it's enough to lock the dog's attention to the area of the marked fall.

The Started field test is fun to judge because you will see the most unexpected happen at any moment. Although we are looking for hunting instinct with enough obedience and training to get by in a hunting situation, the rules should also cover inexperienced and nervous handlers so they know what they are doing. As an example: A young handler came to the *point of origin* (where the dog sits to watch the bird thrown and where the action starts) with a short leash attached to the dog's bright new red collar. When the bird was thrown and the gun fired, the dog went wild to leave the handler's side to make the retrieve. But that could not be done until the handler unhooked the snap from the collar. With the handler's being all thumbs and the dog all paws, the dog's going backward in one direction and the handler in the other, the contest was quickly won by the dog. Out the pup ran with the short leash dragging from the new red collar. Then the pup did an amazing thing: it stopped, picked up the leash in its mouth, then continued its race to the bird. Swooping it up, it then charged back to deliver both bird and leash to its handler.

Although the Started retrieves are simple, the handler should prepare the dog for the specified distances of the tests both on water and on land. Very often the young dogs will hunt short of the falls because they have not been trained to go farther than the distance the handler can throw the

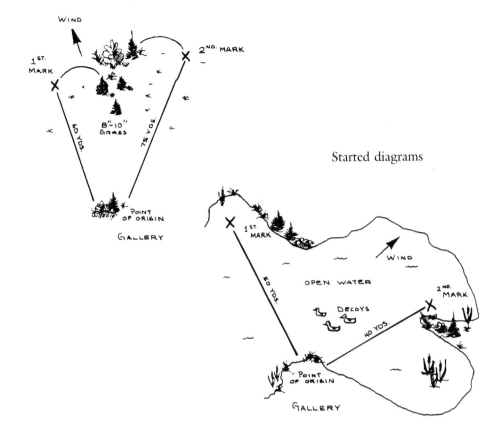

Started diagrams

STARTED, LAND

The Started tests are to demonstrate the dog's basic retrieving instincts. In this test, the judge starts out with a medium-length retrieve of sixty yards. The cover is such that the dog should have no problem. If the dog runs past the bird, the judge will watch to see if the dog turns back to establish an area to hunt. If it does, the wind will help the dog catch the scent. The judge is looking for style and desire. When the dog delivers the first retrieve, it will be given a second single. This appears simple, but it's enough of a test that the judges can find out what they want to know: "Would I like to own this dog? Does it have enough natural ability to take it on through its training?"

STARTED, WATER

In Started the dog can be restrained until the action is over and the bird is down. It is important, and especially in Started, to use attention-getting devices at the point from which the bird is being thrown. Duck calls should be used or blank shots fired. The first bird should produce no problems. The judges will want to see the dog enter the water with the same enthusiasm on the second single. On the second mark, the dog has to ignore the decoys and not be tempted to miss the mark by going up on the point of land to search for the bird. After the two land and two water tests, the judge selects a fifth single-retrieve land or water test; this single retrieve is at the judge's option.

dummy. Gradually, the dog should be extended so that you break any pattern of specific distances. The dog should be given marks that take it from one type of cover to another. Cover changes often work as barriers for a young dog. To teach the dog to use its nose, the marks should be thrown into heavy cover where the dog will not easily see them. You will see by the dog's reaction the instant it gets a snoot full of scent. Many young dogs do not believe their nose, but with practice they learn to use it as well as the eyes.

Training a young dog for the Started field test means that you want it to be eager to retrieve. If it is from good working stock, that desire can be instilled by making retrieving a fun game almost from the day you get the pup at seven weeks. As the dog grows, the distances of these retrieves should be extended. Once they are sufficiently extended, different tests should be set up simulating the field test so that the dog has an idea of what it is all about even before it is entered in an event.

In the NAHRA program, a Started dog receives two and a half points for passing the standard. On receiving five points, the dog receives a Started certificate, and these points may be used toward advanced titles. To pass the standard, the work quality according to the judges has to be 80 percent. There is no age limit in any of the NAHRA categories, and a dog may be run in any of them as many times as the handler wants, but in the Started and Intermediate categories it can only receive its points for awards once. If a handler wishes to keep his dog in the Started category and it passes the standard four times in any one calendar year, he receives the award of a Brass Band. The award is just what it says it is: a brass band to wear on a whistle lanyard.

INTERMEDIATE—THE BIG STEP

Intermediate represents a big step forward in the training of the dog. We would hope that all we wish to see in style and instinct in the Started dog would also show itself in the Intermediate category. An Intermediate dog is a retriever that is trained well enough to be taken on a hunt in any kind of hunting situation, for any kind of game, do a job the hunter would be proud of, and in no way embarrass him in front of his hunting cronies.

The dog will be put to tests of moderate difficulty. They should be the kinds of situations the hunter would encounter on an average day's hunt.

The dog will be required to do a double mark on land (maximum distance one hundred yards) and a double on water (seventy-five yards). This will take training because the second bird to be retrieved in a double requires a certain amount of remembering on the dog's part. The dog will have to demonstrate its ability to quarter a field as it would do on an upland game hunt. Trailing a "crippled" bird will demonstrate its scenting ability and whether it has learned to "believe" its nose. The fifth test is handling to a fifty-yard water blind retrieve.

The judges will be looking for more than natural ability; they will want to see handler control, desire, and teamwork with the handler.

Here the dog must be steady with no help from the handler, and it must deliver to hand. The dog might be required to work from a boat or at some distance from the hunter. Think of a hunting situation, and this dog will be required to do it within the prescribed retrieving distances. The judges will realize that this is not a finished retriever but they always ask themselves the same question: Would I like to hunt with this dog? The tests should be challenging but not tricky. This dog is supposed to do a straightforward working job.

Since the work the dog did in Started depended on the dog's native ability more than on training, there is a big adjustment the new handler has to make in bringing a dog out of the Started class and into the Intermediate. It is going to take time and work to get a young dog to understand double retrieves. The only way to teach it is to do it.

The first doubles a dog should do should be on a grass plot so it can see both falls. The first tests should be widely spread apart, ninety degrees or more. A dog will almost always go to the last bird down first. This will make the memory bird the first dummy thrown. It will be good to keep the first retrieve short and gradually make that memory bird harder and harder. After the dog does this on grass, throw the memory bird into light cover, making the distances longer and longer. Soon you will need a helper in the field to throw the dummy out far enough. Get the dog used to not seeing the thrower and use the attention-getting devices. This should be done in varying kinds of cover, and the dog should learn to be comfortable going into changing cover. Gradually, reduce the angle of the tests so that you end up with a short bird and a long bird almost on the same line. This over-and-under teaches the dog to run through the area and the scent of the first retrieve. These tests must also be done on water.

As you can start to see, the Intermediate field test is no giveaway. Some handlers have asked NAHRA for a category between the Started and Intermediate, but the board has always resisted that suggestion. If the hunter is serious about his dog, he will have to start serious training at some point. Intermediate is it. (These people do not seem to realize that another field test means more judges, bird boys, guns, land, and all the rest of the mechanics of a field event, and that it all costs money. When asked what the tests in such a new category would include, they did not have any real practical suggestions.) You can't get much simpler than Intermediate and have the tests real hunting situations. On further examination of this problem, the board concluded that those who wanted the new category were not seriously training their dogs, or the dogs were from stock that could never do the work. NAHRA is out to separate the working stock from the show stock, the men from the boys—and Intermediate in a very practical way does it.

Many of the people who test their dogs are nonhunters and have a hard time understanding how to teach a dog to quarter a field as in upland hunting. It's a simple affair. The dog does all the learning, and all you have to do is to set it up for it to do it.

The Intermediate dog has had its yard training and should now be well schooled in the COME command. Take the dog to a likely field that has light cover that might very well hold upland birds. Before you take your dog into the field for a "walk," place about six shackled pigeons in different locations. Then start the pup at one end of the field and give it the command HUNT 'EM UP. It will be off for its usual run, looking for all those good places to smell. When it exceeds fifteen yards in front of you (good flushing range for the gun), call it back. We want it to learn that distance. On returning send it off again in a new direction with the HUNT 'EM UP command. You will know when the dog "stumbles" onto the first shackled bird. It will get excited, and its ears and tail will go up. It will "make game," swing around following the smells, and it'll swoop up the pigeon. It is exciting to see a young dog discover bird scent.

Before the dog leaves that field, it learns first of all what wonderful things there are in fields, and the beginnings of learning to stay within flushing range for the gun. In a few lessons, you will see it working out likely cover by getting into it and believing its own nose. It won't be long before you will be walking a straight line through a field, and the dog will be sweeping the cover before you like a windshield wiper.

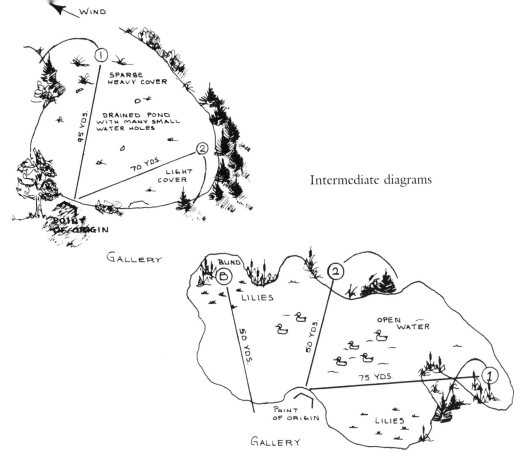

Intermediate diagrams

INTERMEDIATE, LAND

Intermediate is a big step from Started. The dog must be steady at the point of origin with no help from the handler. These will be double retrieves, two birds. A dog on a double retrieve will go for the last bird down first. So it has to remember where the first bird landed and go for it after the retrieve of the second bird. The judges deliberately made that memory bird a longer retrieve. If the dog has forgotten where the bird is, it may be handled by hand signal to the bird. If the dog does a good, crisp job, the judges will give it a good score. The hunter wants his dog back in the blind with the game as quickly as possible.

INTERMEDIATE, WATER

This water work will be divided into two parts, a pair of marks and a blind. The marks show how the dog has been extended. The number-two bird in the marks was thrown on land, so the dog will have to go up on land to make the retrieve. The memory bird was thrown so it is out of sight behind the finger of land. This is a good test since an Intermediate dog is supposed to be able to hunt and not be an embarrassment. The blind water retrieve is short but distant enough for a young dog to demonstrate to the judges that it knows the rudiments of handling.

Trailing is much the same as upland hunting in that the dog learns a good part of the work on its own. You can't teach a dog to use its nose to trail a bird. All you can do is set a trail and let the dog work it out for itself with its nose. There are many ways to lay a trail. The best is to release a pheasant in a field and let the dog follow its trail. Shackle the wings so the bird can't fly and tie a short string between its legs to hobble it so it can't run too fast—or it will be out of the county. Give the bird a five-minute head start and sit back and watch the fun.

Teaching handling, an almost uncanny obedience test, is the work that separates the men from the boys. An Intermediate dog will only have to do a fifty-yard water blind retrieve. But there is no way of faking this test, and there is no way a dog can learn this by itself. The starting point is with the three commands: SIT, STAY, and COME. There is no use trying to teach a dog to obey hand and whistle commands until it is perfect on these three basic commands.

An Intermediate dog will have to know how to take a line and how to play "baseball." As we have said, *Game Dog* gives all the details on how to teach handling, and we won't repeat them here. But here are the elements of the blind retrieve: Of course the dog has no idea where the bird is hidden. The dog is set next to the handler. It is given a general indication with the hand pointing the line to the bird. It is sent in that direction and should continue in a straight line until it either comes upon the bird or is given a whistle command to stop and take a new directional command from the handler. The handler may have to give it a new direction in order to correct the dog's line. Then when the dog gets in the area of the hidden bird it will have to be given hand signals to move it into the range where its nose will zero it in. The dog will have to know "to the right," "to the left," "back," and "come in to me" on the come-in whistle signals.

Intermediate is the most difficult category to judge. The tests must be difficult enough to show the ability of the dog as a hunter but not so difficult that the dogs lack the hunting experience to complete the tasks.

Intermediate is quite a step up from the Started tests, but a title of Working Retriever (WR), which is awarded for the Intermediate work, ʾ ɫ not honestly be made up of anything less than these requirements. A ᵉs the Intermediate standard receives five points toward the WR ᵒn his pedigree. It takes twenty points to earn the title. ɪde by either passing the standard four times or adding ᴀediate scores to the five points won in Started. A dog may continue to run in the Intermediate class as long as it needs, to gain more experience, but no more than the twenty points can be accumulated toward the Senior title.

THE SENIOR DOG

The Senior dog by definition is a finished hunting retriever. It is the elite of all hunting dogs and should show it. This dog is required to do all the work the Intermediate dog must do but without the restrictions. For example, the multiple retrieves on land and water could be triples, and the judge can decide in what order they are to be picked up. There will be both land and water blinds, which can be extended to one hundred yards. In the upland test, there will be a flushed live bird, and the dog will have to stop and be steady to shot and fall, then make the retrieve. Where the Intermediate dog showed that it had acquired the beginning skills as a hunter, the Senior dog will be required to show its hunting experience.

Control is the name of the game in the Senior tests. The word *control* must be explained. The licensed field-trial game also requires control, but it is of a different nature. The blind retrieve can show that difference. When an AKC-licensed field-trial dog is given a line to a blind, it is expected to take a straight line almost indefinitely. Two hundred yards is not out of the ordinary. A NAHRA dog may require two or three whistles to get one hundred yards distance, but if it takes each cast as directed, it is doing the job that is expected of it. This does not mean that one dog is better than the other; it demonstrates the degree of training in that specific area. An AKC dog will go out by water and come back by water: swimming takes a lot of time. A NAHRA dog will go out by water and return by land if that is the quicker way back. The hunter's aim is to recover the birds as fast as possible so the hunting can continue. Another example: The judge gives this scenario to the handler—"Two birds were shot on the water, and the dog is sent to make the first retrieve. When the dog is out about sixty yards, another bird flies in and is shot, winged, and falls fifty yards away and ninety degrees to the side. While swimming, the dog does not see this action; it's a blind retrieve! Get the blind first."

The dog must be stopped and called off the retrieve of the dead bird and sent for the "crippled" bird. This should present no problem for a Senior NAHRA dog. It is doubtful if an AKC field-trial dog could do that; not

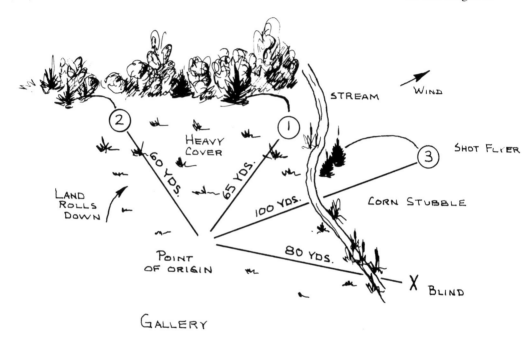

STREAM

WIND

② HEAVY COVER

①

③ SHOT FLYER

60 YDS.

65 YDS.

100 YDS.

CORN STUBBLE

LAND ROLLS DOWN

POINT OF ORIGIN

80 YDS.

X BLIND

GALLERY

SENIOR, LAND

A Senior dog is a finished hunting dog, and whereas we were looking for the beginnings of control in the Intermediate dog, we are looking for near perfect control in the Senior dog. This test is straightforward. It is a triple, and then the blind is run after the marks have been picked up. But the judges could have made the test much harder by changing the throwing sequence and making the long bird, now number three, the number-one bird. It now becomes a long memory bird. Or the judges could use the scenario that all three birds that were thrown for the dog to see were clean kills and the blind is the wounded bird that might get away. So the sequence would be to show the dog the three marked falls, have him ignore them for the moment and do the blind retrieve, get the blind first, then remember the marked falls.

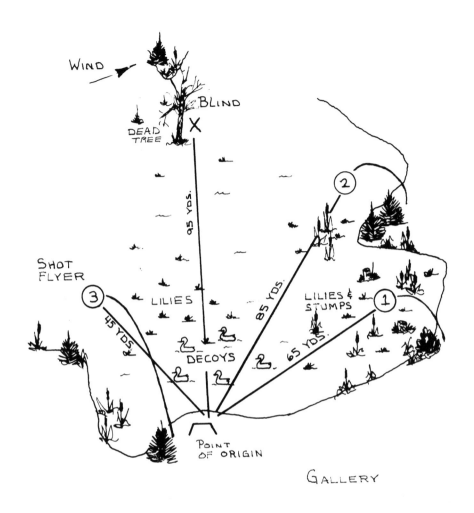

WIND

BLIND

DEAD TREE

X

95 YDS.

②

SHOT FLYER

③

LILIES

85 YDS.

LILIES & STUMPS

①

45 YDS.

DECOYS

65 YDS.

POINT OF ORIGIN

GALLERY

SENIOR, WATER

This Senior water test was used in a recent Invitational. This was in a stick pond with a lot of dead trees and floating logs. The first two birds were thrown, and the dog was sent. It was not easy swimming a straight line because of all the trees and logs. While the dog was returning with the second bird, a "dry" shot was fired. That shot signaled the handler and the dog that a bird had been downed while the dog was swimming and he did not see it go down: a blind retrieve. When the dog delivered the second bird, a live duck (number three) was thrown and shot, landing rather close. This produces great excitement in the dog with all the wing flapping, the flying, and the shots, but the dog must stay under control, ignore that shot bird, and instead go for the blind that it has not seen. After the blind, it still has to remember the shot flyer. That blind retrieve takes a lot of faith and obedience on the dog's part.

because it is not smart enough, but because it is not trained that way. A ninety-degree change of direction is something they are not trained to do. The NAHRA dog is trained to be absolutely under the handler's control, so that when *any* sort of strange hunting situation arises, such as a crippled bird that must be retrieved first, in spite of the fact that the dog was just about to recover a dead bird, the dog can be called off one job and put on another—a NAHRA dog can handle that. AKC field-trial dogs are trained for specific tests. It is miraculous what they can do, but a Senior NAHRA dog is just as spectacular at its work.

The standard that the Senior dog runs against will test its proficiency in both upland and waterfowl hunting for any kind of game in any area in the country. The control that some of the judges expect when they prepare the hunting scenario must keep them up late at night. The dog is awarded twenty points each time he runs the standard with a score of 80 percent or better. A hundred points will confer on the dog a title of Master Hunting Retriever. This is no giveaway. In the first four years, many thousands of dogs have run and there are only ninety MHRs. The title of Grand Master Hunting Retriever—and there are only fifteen after four years of running—is awarded to a dog when it accumulates three hundred points. These are titles that are placed on the dog's pedigree and become very important for the retriever working-dog gene pool.*

The NAHRA
Invitational

The main purpose of the NAHRA program was to save the Labrador and the Golden from the fate of popularity. There is no doubt that the mission impossible has been accomplished as far as the Labrador is concerned. The Golden is another story. The Golden people do not seem to be taking advantage of the NAHRA program. Of the ninety Master Hunting Re-

*The complete NAHRA rule book will best explain the requirements of each category. It can be obtained from the NAHRA office, P.O. Box 6, Garrisonville, VA 22463; 703-752-4000.

triever titles awarded, the Goldens have only seven. We are hoping the message gets out so the Goldens will become more a part of this working-retriever gene pool program. It is really for the protection of the breed's future; otherwise history has shown that the show people will swallow up the breed. As far as the Labrador is concerned, although the NAHRA program is less than five years old, we have enough information in our computers to help anyone almost anywhere in the country to get a working mate for breeding.

NAHRA keeps the records of Started, Intermediate, and Senior dogs that have passed the standards. The program, from the youngest Started dog to the Grand Master, was set up to focus on workability for the gene pool. A Started dog, awarded its certificate, shows that it has the necessary instincts and desire for the work. The dog already indicates that it has the desired working stock in its background. The Intermediate WR denotes that the dog has the right working genes and is trainable. The Senior MHR denotes the cream that comes to the top.

We said in the opening section of this book that the statistics should show us where to find the culprit in this story. It would not take Scotland Yard to figure it out. There is no doubt that the guilty factors are the AKC show ring and the pet market that follows in its wake. We also said that Scotland Yard was not called in because the vigilantes stepped in to solve their own problem. The vigilantes are the NAHRA program and all those that support it. The job has been well done.

As soon as the NAHRA board of directors saw that their objective, to save the work in the dog, was well on its way to success, they turned their attention in a new direction. Although the program was designed for the dog, the board felt that a reward was due all those handlers who became dedicated to the program. The Invitational was conceived.

The Invitational is an annual event. The top Senior dogs in the country are invited to an all-expense-paid, two-day field test. Transportation for the handler and the dog is arranged, and living accommodations are provided. For those who fly in, a four-by-four vehicle is provided for the weekend. There are banquets and tailgate parties and in general a good time for all. But it is a serious business.

The thirty handlers who have acquired the highest number of points with their dogs during the calendar year are invited. This event is only for Senior dogs. All dogs start the year, January 1, with zero points. Every time

The participants are keenly interested . . .

and the dogs love the work.
(Author Photos)

the handler and dog make a team . . .

the handler passes the standard throughout the year his dog receives twenty points. On December 31, the scores are added up. The handlers of the dogs that qualify are notified, and that year's event is held the following May.

This has become the plum, the sought-after prize in retriever circles. You can imagine the competitive spirit the event initiates. The dogs are still not competing against one another. They still work against the standards. Those dogs that pass the standard at the Invitational are named to the NAHRA All-America Team for that year. It's quite an honor!

Index

Page references for illustrations are in **boldface** *type. Commands are shown in* SMALL CAPS.

Woodcock shooting, 92
Work of dogs, 38
  in Newfoundland, 6–7, 51–52
  Newfoundland dog, 47, 48–49
  Newfoundland Water Dog, 83
Working awards, 188
Working breeds
  future of, 172
  ruined by politics, 114
  ruined by show, 123, 124, 127, 172, 223
Working Retriever (WR) title, 186, 218–19
Working Retrievers, The (Quinn), 170

Working stock, 10, 216, 223
World War I, 76
World War II, 28
Wulff, Lee, 20
Wyandanche Club, 134

Yellow Labrador, 9, 10, 82
Yellow Retriever. *See* Golden Retriever
Yellow Russian Retriever. *See* Golden Retriever

Zern, Ed, 181